POSTCARDS 3

Language Booster

Workbook
with Grammar Builder

Brian Abbs
Chris Barker
Ingrid Freebairn

LONGMAN ON THE **WEB**

Longman.com offers online resources for teachers and students. Access our Companion Websites, our online catalog, and our local offices around the world.

Visit us at **longman.com**.

Longman

Postcards 3 Language Booster

Pearson Education, 10 Bank Street, White Plains, NY 10606

Editorial director: Ed Lamprich
Senior development editor: Marilyn Hochman
Development editors: Julie Schmidt, Tunde Dewey
Vice president, director of design and production: Rhea Banker
Executive managing editor: Linda Moser
Production manager: Liza Pleva
Associate managing editor: Mike Kemper
Art director: Ann France
Director of manufacturing: Patrice Fraccio
Senior manufacturing buyer: Nancy Flaggman
Photo research: Aerin Csigay
Cover design: Ann France
Text design: Ann France and Pearson Education Development Group
Text composition: MediaLynx Design Group and Pearson Education
    Development Group
Text font: 11/14 palatino

ISBN: 0-13-093903-X

Printed in the United States of America

10 9 8 7 6 5 4 3 – PBP – 08 07 06 05 04

The authors and publisher wish to acknowledge the contribution of
David McKeegan for writing the activities in the Language Booster.

Illustration credits

pp. 81, 91 Tim Haggerty; pp. 24, 39, 42, 59, 60 Denise Hoff; pp. 22, 34, 58, 66, 74, 77 Michael Hortens; pp. 17, 31, 33, 38, 48, 56, 57, 94, 98, 101 Bart Rivers; pp. 11, 20, 29, 32, 42, 45, 55, 65, 70, 75, 78, 94, 102, 103, 107 Lauren Scheuer; pp. 9, 15, 19, 28, 35, 36, 44, 49, 54, 90, 99, 109 George Thompson; pp. 69, 85, 87, 97, 105, 110 Ron Zalme

Photo credits

p. 10 Powerstock Photo Library; p. 13 AFP/Corbis; p. 23 Bob Daemmrich/The Image Works; p. 24 (top right) Jody Dole/Getty Images, (top left) Courtesy of Chelsea Piers, (middle left) Courtesy of Chelsea Piers, (bottom left) Jerry Marshall; p. 26 (1) Brian Hagiwara/FoodPix, (2) Burke/Triolo Productions/FoodPix, (3) Anthony Johnson/Getty Images, (4) Vincent Besnault/Getty Images, (5) Japack Company/Corbis, (6) John A. Rizzo/Getty Images; p. 40 Myrleen Ferguson Cate/PhotoEdit Inc.; p. 42 (top to bottom) Peter Hayman/Dorling Kindersley Media Library, Liz McAulay/Dorling Kindersley Media Library, Geoff Brightling/ Dorling Kindersley Media Library, National Museum of the American Indian/Smithsonian Institution, Reebok International; p. 50 Don Romero/Index Stock Imagery/PictureQuest; p. 52 (top) Lawrence Migdale/Getty Images, (bottom left) U. S. Census Bureau, (bottom right) Al Messerschmidt/Folio, Inc.; p. 53 The Kobal Collection/The Picture Desk; p. 59 LWA-Dann Tardif/Corbis; p. 60 (top) Columbia/The Kobal Collection, (top middle) Jamie Budge/Corbis, (bottom middle) Warner Bros/The Kobal Collection, (bottom) Zade Rosenthal/Columbia/The Kobal Collection; p. 67 Ebby May/Getty Images; p. 71 Retna Ltd.; p. 73 (left) Spencer Grant/PhotoEdit Inc., (middle) Jack Hollingsworth/ Getty Images, (right) Mike Powell/Getty Images; p. 79 James Randklev/ Getty Images; p. 83 Lori Adamski Peek/Getty Images; p. 86 (top) Walter Bibikow/Index Stock Imagery, (bottom) Kevin Peterson/Getty Images; p. 89 V.C.L./Getty Images; p. 95 AFP/Corbis; p. 106 (top) Tim Hall/ Getty Images, (bottom) Paul Chesley/National Geographic Image Collection.

Welcome to the Language Booster!

This book will give you lots of practice in grammar, vocabulary, and communication skills.

The Workbook

The Language Booster begins with a Workbook section (pages 8–61). It's a workbook with a difference—the exercises in each category (Grammar, Vocabulary, and Communication) are separated into three levels: Getting Started (easy), Moving Up (harder), and Reaching for the Top (challenging). You and your teacher can choose the level that suits you best, or you can work through all the exercises if you like. When you feel confident with one level, you can move on to the next.

After every four units in the Workbook section, there's a Skills Development lesson with an engaging reading. Following the reading are vocabulary, comprehension, and writing activities. In the first reading, you'll read about Chelsea Piers, one of the largest sports centers in the United States. Located in New York City, it offers in-line skating, swimming, wall climbing, and many other exciting activities. In the second reading, you'll read about the wonderful world of shoes—from early Egyptian shoes made from leaves or grass to modern-day running shoes. And in the third reading, you'll read about the difficult—but exciting—work of stunt doubles. (A stunt double fills in for a famous actor during dangerous scenes.)

The Grammar Builder

The second part of the Language Booster is called the Grammar Builder (pages 63–111), and it contains additional grammar exercises. It also includes grammar reference sections called Grammar Highlights so that you can check on grammar rules while you are doing the exercises. You can work through the units in the Grammar Builder simultaneously with the units in the Workbook section, or you can do them at a later stage.

We hope that this Language Booster, with its special features, will give you all the help you need to learn English successfully–and enjoyably.

Scope and Sequence

Workbook

Grammar Builder

Communication	Pages	Grammar
• Introduce oneself to a group.	**64–67**	• Simple present contrasted with the present continuous • Position of adverbs of frequency
• Make suggestions • Express preferences	**68–71**	• Simple past tense: regular and irregular verbs
• Talk about obligations	**72–75**	• *Have to:* simple present and simple past forms
• Express future plans and activities	**76–79**	• The present continuous to express future time • Verb + infinitive
• Order food items and drinks	**80–83**	• *Will* and *won't* for decisions, promises, and future predictions • The imperative
• Describe personalities	**84–87**	• Adjectives and adverbs • *If* clauses to express future meaning

Scope and Sequence

Workbook

Grammar Builder

1 We usually meet at 4:00.

Communication

Getting Started

1 Complete the conversation with the sentences and phrases from the box.

But you can call me Jay.	Yes, I am.	I rarely go to the movies.
~~You're in the 11th grade~~	I always come here	I never play computer
What do you want to see?	Jen for short.	games.
I usually read or chat on the	How often do you	But I often play games
Internet with friends.	come here?	on my computer.

Jason: Hi. _You're in the 11th grade_____, aren't you?
(1)

Jenny: Oh, hi. _____
(2)

Jason: I'm in 11th grade, too. My name's Jason. _____
(3)

Jenny: I'm Jenny. _____
(4)

Jason: That's nice. _____
(5)

Jenny: _____ for a walk after lunch.
(6)

Jason: What do you usually do in the evenings?

Jenny: _____ What about you?
(7)

Jason: Well, I rarely chat on the Internet. _____
(8)

Jenny: Oh. _____
(9)

Jason: Jenny, would you like to go to the movies with me tonight?

Jenny: OK, sure. _____
(10)

Jason: I don't know. What's showing? _____
(11)

Reaching for the Top

2 Imagine that you are meeting a student in a foreign language club. In your notebook, write a conversation between you and this student. Use Exercise 1 as a model.

Grammar

Getting Started

3 Complete the sentences with the simple present or the present continuous form of the verbs in parentheses.

1. I (*take*) ___take___ a shower every morning.

2. She always (*read*) _____ before she (*go*) _____ to sleep.

3. He (*do*) _____ his homework in the kitchen right now.

4. They can't hear you now because they (*watch*) _____ TV, and the volume is too loud.

5. Manuel can't come to the phone right now because he (*chat*) _____ on the Internet.

6. We sometimes (*hang out*) _____ at the mall after school.

4 Who plays video games the most? Read what these people say. Then write their names in order on the lines below, from most to least.

I often play video games after dinner, right before bed.

Yoshi

I sometimes play video games with friends, especially on weekends.

Leon

I never play video games. They're just silly. I prefer to hang out with my friends.

Barbara

I rarely play video games because I'm too busy with other activities.

Lisa

I'm a big fan of video games. I always play for a while after school and again at night before bed.

Larry

___Larry___ _____ _____ _____

5 Unscramble the words to write sentences. Be sure to place the frequency adverbs correctly.

1. work / We / usually / until / five o'clock
   ___We usually work until five o'clock.___

2. Lisa / hangs out / with / her friends / never
   _____

3. frequently / I / go out / on / Saturday nights
   _____

4. visit relatives / sometimes / on weekends / We
   _____

5. rarely / goes / Jason / to / the movies
   _____

6. in school / often / He / is / by 7:30 A.M.
   _____

Moving Up

6 Look at the chart. Write sentences about yourself. Use the cues and adverbs of frequency.

100%	99–90%	89–75%	74–11%	10–1%	0%
always	usually	often	sometimes	rarely	never

1. 100% of the time / I like to be with people.
   I always like to be with people.

2. 0% of the time / I like to be alone.
   _____

3. 90% of the time / I study with friends.
   _____

4. 50% of the time / I study at the library.
   _____

5. 10% of the time / I study alone.
   _____

6. 75% of the time / I go out on Saturday night.
   _____

7 Circle the correct form of the verbs.

Ron Bailey writes newspaper and magazine articles about American music. He (**1.** *likes* / *is liking*) most kinds of music. In the early morning, he (**2.** *listens to* / *is listening to*) a New York radio station that (**3.** *plays* / *is playing*) hits from the 50s, 60s, and 70s. He usually knows the tunes, so he (**4.** *sings* / *is singing*) along with them.

Ron says, "I like world music, too. At the moment, I (**5.** *play* / *am playing*) a CD of African music. It's great. I (**6.** *don't usually listen to* / *am not usually listening to*) classical music, but that's because I (**7.** *don't have* / *am not having*) the time."

Every day at work Ron (**8.** *writes* / *is writing*) about new releases in the pop world. Right now, he (**9.** *does* / *is doing*) a story about a new rock group that (**10.** *record* / *is recording*) its first album.

"Some music is really terrible. I hate it. But that's part of my job. I (**11.** *listen to* / *am listening to*) everything."

Reaching for the Top

8 Write sentences using the cues. Add verbs and other words of your own.

1. I / rarely / after school
   I rarely go to the park after school.

2. We / never / on Saturday morning
   _____

3. My friends / sometimes / at night
   _____

4. My parents / usually / on weekends
   _____

5. Kate / always / in the afternoon
   _____

6. You and I / often / on the Internet
   _____

9 Complete the conversation. Use the simple present or the present continuous form of the verbs in the box. Use contractions when possible. You can use some verbs more than once.

arrive do forget go play practice wait

Tina: Hey, Mario. What (1) _____are_____ you _____doing_____?

Mario: I (2) _____ for tonight's dance. What (3) _____ you _____?

Tina: I (4) _____ for a friend. (5) _____ you _____ every day?

Mario: Not every day. But I always (6) _____ on Saturdays.

Tina: Why?

Mario: My band often (7) _____ at the school dances on Saturday nights. We usually (8) _____ to John's house at about 5:00 P.M. to practice.

Tina: What time (9) _____ you and your band _____ at the dance?

Mario: About 7:30 P.M. (10) _____ you _____ for Sandra?

Tina: Yes, I am. And she's late again! She always (11) _____ about me!

Vocabulary

Getting Started

10 Complete the words with vowels. Write *a, e, i, o,* or *u* in the blanks.

1. w _a_ tch TV
2. t __ lk __ n th __ ph __ n __
3. h __ ng __ __ t w __ th fr __ __ nds
4. r __ __ d m __ g __ z __ n __ s ,
5. ch __ t __ n th __ __ nt __ rn __ t
6. l __ st __ n t __ m __ s __ c

Moving Up

11 Write each phrase from Exercise 10 under the correct picture.

1.

_____watch TV_____

2.

_____

3.

_____

4.

_____

5.

_____

6.

_____

Reaching for the Top

12 Complete the sentences. Use the phrases from Exercise 11. Be sure to use the correct form of the verb in the phrase.

1. I usually _hang out with friends_ at the mall. We have such a good time!

2. Jay _____ because his favorite show is on right now.

3. Every day after school, Mital _____ with her friend about their homework.

4. After dinner, Gary usually _____ with people from around the world.

5. My dad _____ every night. He has hundreds of CDs.

6. I like to _____, but I don't like to read books.

2 It was quite an experience!

Vocabulary

Getting Started

1 Write the words from the box in the puzzle. Which word does not fit? Write it on the line below.

~~big~~	dirty	interesting	poor
busy	efficient	pleasant	ugly

B I G

_____

Moving Up

2 Write the opposite of each adjective.

1. big   _small_
2. interesting   _____
3. ugly   _____
4. pleasant   _____
5. poor   _____
6. dirty   _____
7. efficient   _____
8. busy   _____

Reaching for the Top

3 Complete the sentences with adjectives from the box below.

beautiful	efficient	rich
busy	~~interesting~~	slow
clean	pleasant	uninteresting
dirty		

1. I watched an ___interesting___ TV show last night. I learned a lot!

2. We were very _____ at work today, so I didn't have time to call you.

3. I had a very _____ time yesterday when we had a picnic by the river.

4. We washed my father's car, so it's very _____ now.

5. I think math is the most _____ subject in school. I nearly fall asleep during every lesson!

6. The owner of the world's largest company is a very _____ man.

7. Nicole Kidman is a _____ actress. That's why her poster is on my wall.

8. Please wash your hands. They're _____!

9. Business was _____ today. We didn't have many customers in the store.

10. Our local government is very _____. They finished many new projects quickly this year.

Grammar

Getting Started

4 Complete the sentences with the simple past tense of the verbs in the box.

arrive	enjoy	play	~~visit~~
cook	listen to	try	watch

1. I _visited_ my grandmother in the hospital yesterday afternoon.
2. _____ you _____ that CD I gave you for your birthday?
3. Sandra _____ a wonderful dinner last night.
4. _____ the baseball team _____ well last weekend?
5. They _____ the final episode of *Star Wars* on TV yesterday.
6. Our plane _____ three hours late!
7. _____ the children _____ their trip to the zoo?
8. We _____ to call you last night, but there was no answer.

5 Rewrite the affirmative sentences in the negative and the negative sentences in the affirmative.

1. I didn't see Timothy last night.
   I saw Timothy last night.
2. My parents went to the movies last night.
   My parents didn't go to the movies last night.
3. Jenny had breakfast at 10 A.M.
   _____
4. She took her pet rabbit to school.
   _____
5. Yesterday I didn't go to bed early.
   _____
6. They didn't think it was a good idea.
   _____

7. Mom bought a new dress for the party.
   _____
8. I didn't meet Jeff at 9 P.M.
   _____

Moving Up

6 Complete the sentences. Write the simple past tense of the verbs in parentheses.

Super Star!

Mel Gibson (be) _____was_____ born in
                        (1)
New York State in 1956. In 1968, his father
(take) _____ the family to Australia;
         (2)
Mel (grow) _____ up there. The first movie
              (3)
he (make) _____ was called *Summer City*,
             (4)
but he (become) _____ famous in the
                    (5)
movie *Mad Max* in 1979. He (get) _____
                                      (6)
the part because he looked just right for the role!
He (have) _____ a fight the day before
             (7)
he (meet) _____ the director. He also
             (8)
starred in *Hamlet*, which many of his fans
(not / like) _____ because it wasn't an
                (9)
action movie. But he continued to be very
successful. For the movie *Braveheart,* he
(win) _____ two Oscars, one for directing
         (10)
and one for producing.

He loves jokes. When he was in *Conspiracy Theory,* he (give) _____ his co-star Julia
                               (11)
Roberts an interesting present — a dead rat!

7 **Unscramble the words to write questions about Mel Gibson.**

1. born / was / Mel Gibson / Where
   Where was Mel Gibson born?

2. the family / Who / to Australia / took
   _____

3. the name / was / What / of / his first movie
   _____

4. did / Mel Gibson / famous / become / When
   _____

5. he / Why / get / of "Mad Max" / did / the part
   _____

6. Oscars / win / he / did / How many / for *Braveheart*
   _____

7. was / Mel's / Who / co-star / in *Conspiracy Theory*
   _____

8. give / Mel / What / to his co-star / did
   _____

8 **Write answers to the questions in Exercise 7. Use the information from Exercise 6.**

1. *He was born in New York State.* _____
2. _____
3. _____
4. _____
5. _____
6. _____
7. _____
8. _____

Reaching for the Top

9 **Complete the answers with verbs. Use the correct form.**

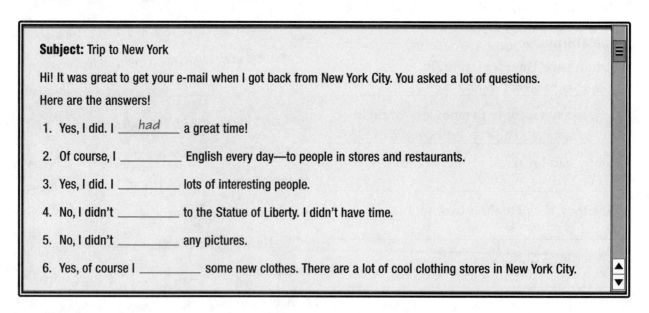

Subject: Trip to New York

Hi! It was great to get your e-mail when I got back from New York City. You asked a lot of questions.
Here are the answers!

1. Yes, I did. I ___*had*___ a great time!

2. Of course, I _____ English every day—to people in stores and restaurants.

3. Yes, I did. I _____ lots of interesting people.

4. No, I didn't _____ to the Statue of Liberty. I didn't have time.

5. No, I didn't _____ any pictures.

6. Yes, of course I _____ some new clothes. There are a lot of cool clothing stores in New York City.

10 **Write the questions for the answers in Exercise 9 in your notebook.**

Example:

1. *Did you have a good time?* _____

Communication

Getting Started

11 Write conversations with *would rather,* *How about . . . ?* or *Why don't we . . .?* and the cues. Use contractions when possible.

1. **Tomas:** (*go / bowling*) How about going bowling?

   Rosa: (*go / the movies*) I'd rather go to the movies.

2. **Tomas:** (*go / shopping*) _____

   Rosa: (*see / a baseball game*) _____

3. **Tomas:** (*watch / TV*) _____

   Rosa: (*go / swimming*) _____

4. **Tomas:** (*have / a barbecue*) _____

   Rosa: (*have / a party*) _____

5. **Tomas:** (*go / horseback riding*) _____

   Rosa: (*stay / at home*) _____

Moving Up

12 Complete the conversation with sentences from the box.

How about hanging out at the mall?	Why don't we go to the beach?	That's a great idea!
~~Hey, why don't we go to the park?~~	I'd rather go to the movies.	The mall is boring.

Tina: I'm bored. Let's do something!

Rob: (1) Hey, why don't we go to the park? _____

Billy: No, I don't feel like going to the park.
(2) _____

Tina: Hmm. I don't feel like going to see a movie. (3) _____
_____

Billy: Nah. (4) _____

Rob: OK, forget the mall. (5) _____
_____

Tina: The beach? (6) _____
_____

Billy: I agree. Let's go to the beach.

Reaching for the Top

13 Imagine that you and two of your friends are discussing what to do after school. In your notebook, write a conversation. Use Exercise 12 as a model.

3 Do I have to?

Vocabulary

Getting Started

1 Match the household chores in Column A with a word or phrase in Column B. Write the letters.

	A		B
_b_	1. cook	a.	the clothes
____	2. vacuum	b.	dinner
____	3. iron	c.	my room
____	4. make	d.	the dishes
____	5. wash	e.	the floor
____	6. clean	f.	the table
____	7. clear	g.	my bed

Moving Up

2 Complete the sentences with the household chores from Exercise 1. Use the correct form of the verbs.

1. The last time I _ironed the clothes_, I burned a hole in my shirt.

2. Anita _____ every night because she gets home early.

3. I _____ as soon as I get out of it.

4. I usually _____, and my brother usually dries them.

5. My mother always tells me to _____ because she thinks it's a mess.

6. After dinner we _____ because we wanted to play board games on it.

Reaching for the Top

3 Complete the questions in the survey below. Then write true and complete answers.

Household Chore Survey

1. _Do you do_ the laundry?
   No, I don't. My father usually does
   it, but I sometimes help.

2. _____ the grocery shopping?
   _____

3. _____ your bed every day?
   _____
   _____

4. _____ your clothes?
   _____

5. How often _do you clean_ your room?
   I clean it once a week.

6. How often _____ breakfast for your family?
   _____

7. How often _____ the floor?
   _____

8. How often _____ the dishes?
   _____

Grammar

Getting Started

4 Circle the correct answers in the conversations.

1. A: Do you (*have to* / *has to*) go now?

   B: Yes. I (*have to* / *has to*) be at work by 9 A.M.

2. A: Does Kunio (*have to* / *has to*) stay home today?

   B: Yes, he does. He (*have to* / *has to*) clean his room.

3. A: Do we (*have to* / *has to*) wash the dishes?

   B: No, we don't. My little brother (*have to* / *has to*) wash them today.

4. A: Does Yoko (*have to* / *has to*) cook any meals today?

   B: Yes, she does. She (*have to* / *has to*) cook dinner tonight.

5. A: Does Gail (*have to* / *has to*) be home by 10 P.M.?

   B: No, she doesn't. But she (*have to* / *has to*) be home by midnight.

5 Unscramble the words to write sentences.

1. last year / dentist / had to / I / see / the

   I had to see the dentist last year.

2. until 6 P.M. / work / had to / Elaine

   _____

3. study / had to / I / last weekend

   _____

4. reporter / write a story / every day / The / had to

   _____

5. clear / waiter / had to / the table / The

   _____

6. clean his room / Masa / had to / once a week

   _____

Moving Up

6 Write a sentence about each picture. Use *has to*, *have to*, or *had to* and the cues.

1.

(*Carmen*) _____ Carmen has to stop. _____

2.

(*Yesterday / the boys*) _____

_____

3.

(*At 10 A.M. this morning / Neil*) _____

_____

4.

(*We*) _____ every day.

5.

(*Esin and Rashida / always*) _____

_____ twice a week.

7 Complete the sentences with the correct form of *have to.*

1. Alex ___didn't have to___ do his homework because it was Friday night.

2. We _____ go home early because we had school the next day.

3. _____ you _____ vacuum the floor last night?

4. Yesterday I _____ call my cousin because it was her birthday.

5. They _____ bring a cake to the party because we already had one.

6. _____ your sister _____ iron the clothes last weekend?

Reaching for the Top

8 Make sentences. Choose a word or phrase from Column A and a phrase from Column B. Use *has to, have to, doesn't have to,* and *don't have to.*

A	B
Nurses	serve food in a restaurant.
A waiter	carry people's luggage up to their rooms.
Administrative assistants	find rooms for hotel guests.
	answer the phone.
A hotel receptionist	train every day.
Professional athletes	look after people in hospitals.

1. *Nurses have to look after people in hospitals.*
2. *A waiter doesn't have to train every day.*
3. _____
4. _____
5. _____
6. _____
7. _____
8. _____
9. _____
10. _____

9 Complete the conversation. Use the simple past form of *have to* and the pronoun and the verb in parentheses.

Joanna: When you first started working, Grandma, what time (*you / get up*)

___did you have to get up___ ?
(1)

Mrs. Elliot: At five o'clock in the morning.

Joanna: That's early!

Mrs. Elliot: That's right. (*I / get up*)

_____ early to get the
(2)
train into town.

Joanna: So what time (*you / start*)

_____ work?
(3)

Mrs. Elliot: At 7:30 A.M. during the week and at 8 A.M. on Saturdays.

Joanna: On Saturdays?

Mrs. Elliot: Yes, (*we / work*) _____ on
(4)
Saturday mornings, but (*we / not work*) _____ on Saturday
(5)
afternoons.

Joanna: What kind of work (*you / do*)

_____ ?
(6)

Mrs. Elliot: (*I / type*) _____ letters and
(7)
(*I / answer*) _____ the
(8)
phone. But (*I / not make*)

_____ the coffee!
(9)

Communication

Getting Started

10 Amanda is interviewing Mike about household chores. Complete the conversation. Use Amanda's notes to help you.

> **Interview with Mike**
>
> —wash the dishes?   —twice a week
> —make your bed?   —every day
> —cook dinner?   —no
> —clean your room?   —once a month
> —do laundry?   —never

Amanda: Mike, do you have to wash the dishes at home?

Mike: Yes, I do. I (1) *have to wash the dishes twice a week.*

Amanda: (2) _____

Mike: Yes, I do. Every day.

Amanda: Do you have to cook dinner?

Mike: (3) _____

Amanda: (4) _____

Mike: Yes, I do.

Amanda: (5) _____

Mike: Once a month.

Amanda: Do you have to do the laundry?

Mike: (6) _____

Moving Up

11 Read Amanda's notes from her interview with Janet. Then, in your notebook, write their conversation. Use Exercise 10 as a model.

> **Interview with Janet**
>
> —wash the dishes?   —every day
> —make your bed?   —no
> —cook dinner?   —twice a week
> —clean your room?   —no
> —do laundry?   —once a month

Amanda: *Janet, do you have to wash the dishes at home?*

Janet: *Yes, I do. . . .*

Reaching for the Top

12 Imagine that Amanda is interviewing you about the household chores you have to or don't have to do. In your notebook, write the conversation.

Who's going to the game?

Grammar

Getting Started

1 **Complete the sentences. Write the verbs in parentheses in the present continuous for the future. Use contractions when possible.**

1. (*I / see*) ___I'm seeing___ my mother tomorrow.
2. (*he / play*) _____ golf on Friday.
3. (*they / not come*) _____ to the party on Saturday.
4. (*we / watch*) _____ TV tonight.
5. (*you / go*) _____ shopping later?
6. (*she / give*) _____ an interview at six.
7. (*he / not go*) _____ skating.
8. (*she / come*) _____ for dinner?
9. (*they / buy*) _____ a computer this Christmas.
10. (*she / fly*) _____ to Paris at 8:30 P.M.

2 **Complete the sentences with the infinitive form of the verbs from the box.**

buy	give up	jump off	listen to	practice
do	go to	~~learn~~	meet	teach

Last week my girlfriend told me that she

wanted ___to learn___ how to skateboard.
                (1)

I offered _____ her, and we agreed
              (2)

_____ by the statue in the park at 4:30 P.M.
   (3)

I brought my skateboard along. She couldn't do

it at first, but she refused _____ and soon
                                      (4)

she was skateboarding around the park. "I'm

going to try _____ some tricks now!" she
                   (5)

said to me. But I told her she needed

_____ for a few more weeks before she
   (6)

could try anything fancy. Unfortunately, she

refused _____ me and decided _____
            (7)   (8)

the path and onto the grass. She fell and hurt

her leg. "Would you like me _____ you a
                                    (9)

skateboard for your birthday next week?"

I asked her. "No, thanks," she replied. "I think

I'd prefer _____ a nice restaurant."
               (10)

Moving Up

3 Read Isabel's diary for next week. Write *Yes/No* questions and short answers about her plans. Use the diary and the cues.

```
Isabel's Diary

Sunday      wash hair
Monday      go to movies with
            my friends
Tuesday     meet Jake for coffee
Wednesday   play tennis with Mike
Thursday    go shopping with
            my sister
Friday      go to Jim's party
Saturday    buy present for
            my mother
```

1. hair / Sunday?

   Is she washing her hair on Sunday?

   Yes, she is.

2. Jim's party / Saturday?

   Is she going to Jim's party on Saturday?

   No, she isn't.

3. movies with her friends / Monday?

   _____

   _____

4. Jake for coffee / Wednesday?

   _____

   _____

5. shopping with her sister / Thursday?

   _____

   _____

6. tennis with Mike / Tuesday?

   _____

   _____

7. present for her mother / Saturday?

   _____

   _____

4 Unscramble the words to write questions about Isabel's plans.

1. she / is / What / on Sunday / doing

   What is she doing on Sunday?

2. going / she / Where / on Monday / is

   _____

3. meeting / Who / she / is / on Tuesday

   _____

4. tennis / playing / is / she / When

   _____

5. doing / on Thursday / is / she / What

   _____

6. going / on Friday / Where / she / is

   _____

5 In your notebook, write answers to the questions in Exercise 4. Use the information from Isabel's diary in Exercise 3.

Example:

1. *She's washing her hair on Sunday.*

Reaching for the Top

6 In your notebook, write three things that you are doing this weekend. Then write three things that you aren't doing this weekend.

Examples:

   I'm visiting my friend.

   I'm not going to see a movie.

7 Complete the sentences with true information about yourself. Use the infinitive form.

1. I would like *to live in Canada*, but I wouldn't like _____.

2. Once, I forgot _____.

3. I can afford _____, but I can't afford _____.

4. One day I hope _____.

5. I need _____, but I don't need _____.

Vocabulary

Getting Started

8 Circle the names of eight sports in the puzzle. Look across, down, and diagonally.

```
B O (R U N N I N G) V
U A F R I N K O L O
B A S E B A L L U L
A F O K T G I T P L
W A C N E R O M I E
F O C L N T E L N Y
T R E N N I B O F B
I N R A I L O A U A
P R A N S E R O L L
S W I M M I N G A L
```

Moving Up

9 Write the names of the sports from Exercise 8 under the correct picture.

1. ____running____   2. _____

3. _____   4. _____

5. _____   6. _____

7. _____   8. _____

Reaching for the Top

10 Write the names of the sports from Exercise 9 in the correct columns.

Field	Course	Track	Court	Pool
		running		

Communication

Getting Started

11 Number the lines of the conversation in the correct order.

_____ What are you doing on Saturday evening?

_____ Yes. That would be great. Thanks.

_____ Yes, I'm very busy. I'm going out on Tuesday, and I'm playing in a volleyball match on Thursday.

_____ Because I have two tickets for a baseball game on Saturday. Do you want to come?

__1__ Are you doing anything next week?

_____ Saturday? I'm not doing anything on Saturday. Why?

12 In your notebook, write the conversation from Exercise 11 in the correct order.

Example:

A: _Are you doing anything next week?_

B: _____

Moving Up

13 Write a conversation using the cues and the present continuous.

A: you / do / on Saturday?

(1) _What are you doing on Saturday?_

B: visit / Grandma / at the hospital / I / afternoon

(2) _____

_____

A: you / do / morning?

(3) _____

_____

B: Nothing.

A: I / go / basketball game

(4) _____

_____

B: anyone else / go?

(5) _____

_____

A: Yes, / Martha / go / too

(6) _____

_____

B: Cool.

Reaching for the Top

14 Imagine that you are inviting a friend to go to a sports event with you. Your friend can't go this weekend, but he or she can go next weekend. Write the conversation in your notebook. Use the conversation in Exercise 11 as a model.

You: _Are you doing anything this weekend?_

Friend: _Yes, . . ._

Skills Development 1

Reading

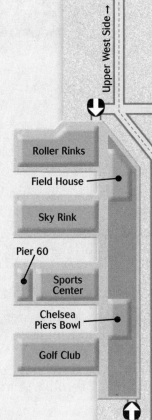

Something for Everyone

Chelsea Piers is one of the biggest sports centers in the United States. It's in New York City, a few blocks from the Empire State Building. The builders of this sports complex started with four piers in the Hudson River. In the past, boats going to Europe and South America came to these piers every day. Now thousands of people come and go, looking for a place to exercise, relax, and enjoy themselves.

There is something for everyone at Chelsea Piers. Do you like in-line skating? Just visit the **Roller Rinks**. You'll find outdoor rinks for relaxed family skating or exciting team-skating sports. There is also a skating school where you can learn how to skate. For challenging skating, visit the Extreme Park at the Roller Rinks. You can also ride your mountain bike at the Extreme Park.

If you like swimming, try the **Sports Center**. There is a 25-yard, 6-lane swimming pool overlooking the Hudson River. Would you like to try a different sport? In the same building there is a running track, a climbing wall, and basketball courts. The building even has a café where you can relax and enjoy a beverage after you finish exercising.

Step out the front door of the Sports Center and what do you see? A bowling alley! In fact, **Chelsea Piers Lanes** contains forty bowling alleys. They're open until 2 A.M. and serve food and beverages.

Don't leave Chelsea Piers without stopping at the **Field House**. There you can play soccer, practice gymnastics, or even take a dance lesson. Would you like to learn how to play baseball? There are four batting cages where you can practice.

At the end of the day, many visitors enjoy a boat ride on the Hudson River. At **Pier 60** you can choose from several rides. Get on the *Chelsea Screamer* and explore New York City from the water. Your group can choose where it wants to go and can plan an exciting day or night trip. Or take a Spirit Cruise and enjoy a quiet dinner on the water. Before you leave Chelsea Piers, take a walk down the mile-long **Pier Park** and watch the boats go by as the sun sets over the river. Maybe you'd like to come back tomorrow.

Upper West Side →

Roller Rinks

Field House

Sky Rink

Pier 60

Sports Center

Chelsea Piers Bowl

Golf Club

Greenwich Village →

Vocabulary

1 **Complete the sentences with words from the box.**

court	cage	lanes	track
rink	wall	alley	

1. You play basketball on a ___court___ .

2. An ice-skating _____ is an area of ice where people can skate.

3. You can practice hitting a baseball in a _____ .

4. There is a _____ for people to climb in the Sports Center.

5. The swimming pool is divided into _____ .

6. In the Olympics, the running events take place on a _____ .

7. There are forty lanes in the bowling _____ .

Comprehension

2 **Read the sentences. Are they true or false? Circle *T* for true or *F* for false.**

1. (T) F   Chelsea Piers is along the Hudson River.

2. T F   You can swim at Chelsea Piers.

3. T F   People go to Chelsea Piers to play tennis.

4. T F   You can skate outdoors at Chelsea Piers.

5. T F   You can take skating lessons at Chelsea Piers.

6. T F   The Sports Center does not have a café.

7. T F   You can learn how to play baseball at Chelsea Piers.

8. T F   Boats to Europe and South America still leave from the Chelsea Piers today.

3 **Look at the activities in the box below. Write each activity in the correct column in the chart.**

learn how to skate	take a boat ride
run on a track	play basketball
go in-line skating	play soccer
learn how to dance	climb a wall
ride a mountain bike	swim
practice hitting a baseball	

Roller rinks	Sports center	Field house	Pier 60
learn how to skate			

Writing

4 **Imagine your ideal sports and entertainment center. Write a paragraph describing it in your notebook.**

Example:

My ideal sports and entertainment center has

tennis courts because I love tennis. It also has

a movie theater so people can watch movies

after they exercise. . . .

5 I'll have a sandwich.

Vocabulary

Getting Started

1 Find the names of the food items. Match a word or phrase in Column A with a word in Column B. Write the letters.

	A		B
_d_	1. New York	a.	platter
____	2. chicken noodle	b.	salad
____	3. orange	c.	soup
____	4. seafood	d.	steak
____	5. chocolate	e.	cake
____	6. mixed green	f.	juice
____	7. grilled	g.	chicken

Moving Up

2 Complete the names of the food items. Write *a, e, i, o,* or *u* in the blanks.

1. _i_ c _e_ c r _e_ _a_ m
2. m __ l k
3. p __ s t __ s p __ c __ __ l
4. b __ t t l __ d w __ t __ r
5. p __ d d __ n g
6. c h __ __ s __ c __ k __
7. v __ g __ t __ b l __ s __ __ p

3 Write the name of each food item from Exercise 2 under the correct picture. One food item does not have a picture!

 1.
 2.
 3.

vegetable soup   _____   _____

 4.
 5.
6.

_____   _____   _____

4 Write each word from the box next to its definition.

stomp	shake	~~hop~~	rock
slide	kick	spin	

1. To jump up and down on one foot   _hop_
2. To move something very quickly up and down, and from side to side   _____
3. To put your foot down hard and quickly   _____
4. To move smoothly across something   _____
5. To turn around and around very quickly   _____
6. To move one foot up very quickly   _____
7. To move slowly back and forth or from side to side   _____

Reaching for the Top

5 Design a menu for your ideal restaurant. Use the food items you learned in this unit.

BISTRO MENU

Soups

_____

_____

Salads

_____

_____

Entrées
(Main Courses)

_____

_____

Drinks

_____

_____

Desserts

_____

_____

Grammar

Getting Started

6 Complete the sentences. Write *will* or *won't* and an appropriate verb. Use contractions when possible.

1. A: The movie starts in two hours.

   B: Great! We _____'ll have_____ time to eat dinner first!

2. A: Look at the time!

   B: Don't worry. We _____ late.

3. A: I'm worried about the exam.

   B: Relax. You _____ fine.

4. A: I would love to visit Brazil.

   B: Well, we _____ next summer, if you want.

5. A: It's almost eleven o'clock.

   B: Don't worry. We _____ there soon.

6. A: I don't have any warm clothes.

   B: That's OK. It _____ very cold.

Moving Up

7 Look at Tim's schedule. Write questions and answers about his travels. Use the simple future with *will* and *won't* and the cues. Use contractions when possible.

APPOINTMENTS

April 13–20: Rio de Janeiro

April 21–May 5: London

May 6–May 20: Cairo

May 21–June 6: Hong Kong

June 7–June 30: Sydney

July 1–July 10: San Francisco

1. Rio de Janeiro / April 21

   Will he be in Rio de Janeiro on April 21?

   No, he won't. He'll be in London.

2. Cairo / May 15

   _____

   _____

3. London / May 6

   _____

   _____

4. Hong Kong / June 16

   _____

   _____

5. Sydney / July 1

   _____

   _____

6. San Francisco / July 9

   _____

   _____

Reaching for the Top

8 Unscramble the words to write questions. Then write true answers about yourself.

1. you / be / will / Where / morning / tomorrow

    Where will you be tomorrow morning?

    I'll be in bed.

2. after / you / What / do / will / school

    _____

3. eat dinner / you / tonight / will / Where

    _____

4. you / Who / see / this evening / will

    _____

5. sixty years old / be / you / will / When

    _____

9 Diego and his mother Ana are talking about things he wants to do. Complete Ana's commands using the cues and affirmative or negative imperatives.

1. **Diego:** I want to call my friend at six o'clock in the morning.

    Ana: No. *Don't call your friend at six o'clock in the morning.*

2. **Diego:** I want to eat chocolate cake for breakfast.

    Ana: No. _____

    _____

3. **Diego:** I want to stay in bed until 1 P.M. on Saturday.

    Ana: OK. _____

    _____

4. **Diego:** I want to use a dictionary when I do my English homework.

    Ana: OK. _____

    _____

5. **Diego:** I want to take my cell phone to the movies.

    Ana: No. _____

    _____

6. **Diego:** I want to join the volleyball team at school.

    Ana: OK. _____

    _____

10 Complete the sentences with the verbs from the box. Use the cues and affirmative or negative imperatives.

| hurry up   close   take   cry   ~~walk~~ |

1. (*not*) ___Don't walk___ on the grass!

2. Please _____ the window. It's cold in here.

3. _____ one tablet, three times a day.

4. Please (*not*) _____. Everything will be OK.

5. _____. We'll be late!

Communication

Getting Started

11 Unscramble the words to write questions.

1. for / Anything / dessert

   Anything for dessert?

2. specials / What / today's / are

   _____

3. would / to / you / What / like / drink

   _____

4. Are / ready / to / order / you

   _____

Moving Up

12 Complete the conversation. Use the questions from Exercise 11.

Server: Hello. (1) *Are you ready to order?*

Ren: Yes, we are. (2) _____

Server: We have New York steak and a pasta special.

Ren: Hmm. I think I'll have a spinach salad.

Yoko: And I'll have a hamburger and a slice of cheesecake.

Server: One spinach salad, one hamburger, and a slice of cheesecake. And you, sir? (3) _____

Ren: No, thanks. I'll just have the salad.

Server: (4) _____

Ren: Bottled water, please.

Yoko: Me, too.

Reaching for the Top

13 Imagine that you and a friend are in a restaurant. Write a conversation you both have with the server on the lines below. Use the conversation in Exercise 12 as a model.

_____

_____

_____

_____

_____

_____

_____

_____

_____

_____

_____

_____

6

If you need me, I'll be there.

Vocabulary

Getting Started

1 Match each word in Column A with its definition in Column B. Write the letters.

A	B
_d_ 1. loyal	a. good at doing useful things
___ 2. honest	b. careful
___ 3. patient	c. never tells lies
___ 4. cautious	d. is always a friend
___ 5. considerate	e. is happy to wait
___ 6. practical	f. thinks of others

2 Add *dis-*, *im-*, *in-*, or *un-* to the words in the box to make their opposites. Then write them in the correct column.

predictable	practical	~~loyal~~	patient
considerate	decisive	honest	kind

dis-		in-	
1. _disloyal_		5. _____	
2. _____		6. _____	
im-		**un-**	
3. _____		7. _____	
4. _____		8. _____	

Moving Up

3 Write the definitions for the words in the columns in Exercise 2.

1. _____   5. _____
2. _____   6. _____
3. _____   7. _____
4. _____   8. _____

Reaching for the Top

4 Read each statement. Choose a word from the box that best describes the person who made the statement. Write the word on the line.

sincere	disrespectful	sensible
shy	~~inconsiderate~~	polite

1. "I don't care if I hurt other people, as long as I have fun."   _inconsiderate_

2. "I always interrupt people when they talk."   _____

3. "I really hope you do well on your exams. I really do."   _____

4. "Excuse me. May I ask you a question, please?"   _____

5. "I never buy anything I can't afford."   _____

6. "I'm afraid to talk to people I don't know."   _____

Grammar

Getting Started

5 Circle the correct words.

1. Sally is a (*great* / *greatly*) tennis player.
2. She always beats her boyfriend (*easy* / *easily*).

3. Sally's boyfriend plays soccer very (*bad* / *badly*).
4. He isn't a very (*good* / *well*) tennis player either.

5. Sally always drives (*careful* / *carefully*).
6. She is (*patient* / *patiently*) with other drivers.

7. Sally's boyfriend is in a rock band. He is a (*loud* / *loudly*) singer.
8. He never plays his guitar (*soft* / *softly*).

6 Complete the sentences. Write the correct form of the verbs in parentheses.

1. If you (*work*) __work__ hard, you (*be*) __will be__ successful.
2. Yuki (*go*) _____ to the movies if she (*finish*) _____ her homework in time.
3. If Mr. Chou (*not / get*) _____ that new job, he (*not / be*) _____ very happy.
4. Javier (*give*) _____ Mary Ann flowers for her birthday if he (*be*) _____ considerate.
5. Isabel (*go*) _____ to the party if Leo (*ask*) _____ her.
6. If Ying (*not / feel*) _____ comfortable, she (*not / play*) _____ the piano at her friend's wedding.

Moving Up

7 Rewrite the sentences. Change the adjectives to adverbs.

1. She is a terrible cook.
   *She cooks terribly.*_____
2. He is a fast runner.
   _____
3. She's a good volleyball player.
   _____
4. They are hard workers.
   _____
5. My dog is a very noisy eater.
   _____
6. It was easy for us to win.
   _____

8 Complete the sentences with verbs from the box. Write the correct form of the verb. Use contractions when possible.

buy	~~leave~~	find	be	pass	visit	watch

1. If you _____don't leave_____ now, you'll miss your train.

2. If you lose your umbrella, I _____ you a new one.

3. If Peter studies hard, he _____ his exam.

4. If they eat a big lunch, they _____ hungry this afternoon.

5. If there's nothing good on TV, we _____ a video instead.

6. If she _____ her family in England this year, she'll do it next year.

7. If I _____ that book you're looking for, I'll send it to you.

Reaching for the Top

9 Complete the sentences with true information about yourself. Use contractions when possible.

1. If I finish my homework early tonight, _I'll go out_ _____.

2. I'll be very angry if _____.

3. Marina will come to the party if _____.

4. My mother will be happy if _____.

5. If you don't exercise, _____.

6. If it's sunny tomorrow, _____.

7. If _____, you'll get into trouble.

8. If I save a lot of money, _____.

9. If I forget my dad's birthday, _____.

10. If my dad forgets my birthday, _____.

11. We won't go to the soccer game if _____.

12. If _____, they won't go to the baseball game.

Moving Up

10 Complete the conversation with sentences from the box.

> Is he handsome?
> Funny, huh? That's important.
> He sounds too good to be true!
> What about his personality?
> ~~Really? What's his name?~~
> What will you do if he says no?

Tara: Hey, Tina, guess what? I really like this new guy in my class!

Tina: (1) _____ *Really? What's his name?* _____

Tara: Steven.

Tina: (2) _____

Tara: Yes, he is.

Tina: (3) _____

Tara: Oh, he's really lively and funny.

Tina: (4) _____

Tara: Yeah . . . I'm going to call him tonight and ask him to take me out.

Tina: (5) _____

Tara: He won't. He's really considerate. And he's crazy about me!

Tina: (6) _____

Reaching for the Top

11 In your notebook, write a conversation between two teenage boys. One boy is describing a new girl in his class to the other boy. He has a crush on this girl. Use the conversation in Exercise 10 as a model.

7 Have you seen these fashions?

Vocabulary

Getting Started

1 Look at the pictures. Then unscramble the letters to write the names of the different clothes and personal possessions.

1.  s o s h t r   <u>shorts</u>

2. t e r s e w a   _____

3. s r e d s   _____

4. o p t   _____

5.  s n a p t   _____

6.  k r i t s   _____

7.  r e a n r i g s   _____

8.  s k e a n s r e   _____

9. a j t c k e   _____

Moving Up

2 Cross out the word that does not belong in the group.

1. shorts, ~~socks~~, pants, jeans
2. coat, jacket, skirt, sweater
3. wallet, watch, earrings, necklace
4. purse, briefcase, wallet, dress
5. sandals, shoes, stockings, sneakers

Reaching for the Top

3 Complete the sentences. Write the names of the clothes or personal possessions.

1. Many businessmen carry their papers in a ____<u>briefcase</u>____.

2. If you don't wear a _____, your pants will fall down.

3. My girlfriend keeps her makeup in her _____.

4. I keep money, credit cards, and my driver's license in my _____.

5. You wear a _____ on your wrist to tell the time.

6. A _____ is a piece of jewelry you wear around your neck.

7. It's uncomfortable to wear shoes without _____.

Communication

Getting Started

4 Complete the conversations with sentences from the box.

> Yeah, right.
> No, thanks. We're just looking.
> I wouldn't be caught dead wearing that.
> ~~Yes, please. Do you have this shirt in black?~~
> No, I haven't.

1.

   A: Do you need any help?
   B: *Yes, please. Do you have this shirt in black?*

2.

   A: What do you think of this dress?
   B: _____

3.

   A: Do you need any help?
   B: _____

4.

   A: Have you tried these on yet?
   B: _____

5.

   A: I'm the most fashionable girl in school!
   B: _____

Moving Up

5 Number the lines of the conversation in the correct order. Then write the conversation in the correct order on the lines below.

Clerk

___ I'm sure we do. What size are you?

___ Sure, the dressing room is behind you.

___ We have some dresses over here.

_1_ Do you need any help?

___ Here you go.

Judy

___ Let's see. Do you have this one in red?

___ May I try it on?

___ Small, please.

___ Yes, I'm looking for a party dress.

Clerk: *Do you need any help?*

Judy: _____

Clerk: _____

Judy: _____

Clerk: _____

Judy: _____

Clerk: _____

Judy: _____

Clerk: _____

Reaching for the Top

6 Imagine that you are in a clothing store looking for a dress or a pair of pants. In your notebook, write a conversation between you and a salesperson. Use the conversation in Exercise 5 as a model.

Grammar

Getting Started

7 Match the base form of each verb with its past participle. Write the letters.

Base form	Past participle
_f_ 1. call	a. bought
____ 2. have	b. left
____ 3. buy	c. seen
____ 4. see	d. worn
____ 5. stop	e. lived
____ 6. leave	f. called
____ 7. meet	g. known
____ 8. know	h. had
____ 9. live	i. met
____ 10. wear	j. stopped

8 Complete each sentence with a verb from Exercise 7. Write the present perfect form of the verb.

1. Look! Someone __has left__ a briefcase on the bus.

2. _____ you always _____ your bread in this bakery?

3. I _____ already _____ this movie.

4. Listen. I think it _____ raining.

5. Sara _____ the same dress for the last three days!

6. I _____ their office many times, but no one is ever there.

7. I _____ a cold since last week.

8. _____ you _____ my sister Susan?

9. They _____ each other for seven years.

10. Stanley _____ in this town since he was a baby.

Moving Up

9 Unscramble the words to write statements or questions.

1. played / never / I / have / tennis
   I have never played tennis.

2. you / heard / about / car / new / Sally's / Have
   _____

3. you / How long / that book / have / had
   _____

4. have / You / your homework / done / not
   _____

5. you / Have / ever / been / to his house
   _____

6. have / that dress / worn / I
   _____

Reaching for the Top

10 Write questions and short answers. Use the cues and the present perfect tense.

1. you / ever / be / to Spain

   Have you ever been to Spain?

   Yes, __I have__ .

2. you / cook / dinner / our

   _____

   No, _____ .

3. your brother / meet / my sister

   _____

   Yes, _____ .

4. you / clean / your room

   _____

   Yes, _____ .

5. they / ever / have / an argument

   _____

   No, _____ .

6. shop / there / you / many times

   _____

   Yes, _____ .

11 Write true sentences about your experiences and your friend's. Use the present perfect and the cues from the box.

eat / snails	be / in a car accident
wear / a hat	see / Marc Anthony
grow / a garden	go / bungee jumping

1. _I have never eaten snails._

   My friend has eaten snails.

2. _____

   _____

3. _____

   _____

4. _____

   _____

5. _____

   _____

6. _____

   _____

Study Corner

Using *for* and *since* with the Present Perfect

Use *for* and a length of time to say how long a situation has lasted.

*I have lived in this house **for** two years.*

Use ***since*** and a point in time to say when something began.

*I have lived in this house **since** 2001.*

12 Complete the sentences with *for* or *since*.

1. They have known each other __for__ years.

2. He hasn't traveled _____ March.

3. I have studied English _____ five years.

4. We have wanted to see this movie _____ last week.

5. She has been asleep _____ two hours.

6. I've been in this country _____ 1982.

8 He's the one who gave him a D.

Vocabulary

Getting Started

1 Look at the sentences in Column A. Match them with the sentences that have the same meaning in Column B. Write the letters.

A	B
b 1. I did OK on my exam.	a. Marcia almost failed that teacher's class.
___ 2. I hope I get Mr. Lowe next year.	b. My grade on the test was pretty good.
___ 3. That teacher gave Marcia a D+.	c. Who's your science teacher?
___ 4. Who do you have for science?	d. I hope Mr. Lowe will be my teacher next year.

Moving Up

2 Complete the conversations. Choose your responses from the box.

> Who's your history teacher?
> I hope *I* don't get Mr. Newman next year.
> ~~I did OK on my test.~~
> She almost failed her class.

1. A: How did you do on your test?
   B: *I did OK on my test.* _____

2. A: _____
   B: Ms. Mangan.

3. A: How did Laura do in her class?
   B: _____

4. A: I have Mr. Newman this year. He's very strict and demanding.
   B: _____

Grammar

Getting Started

3 Match the two parts of each sentence. Write the letters on the lines.

d 1. I know an artist	a. that we will visit tomorrow.
___ 2. Reiko has done some paintings	b. who loves to go to museums.
___ 3. You can see her work in the museum	c. where they have delicious soup.
___ 4. It's in the neighborhood	d. who is famous.
___ 5. I went with a friend	e. where I live.
___ 6. We had lunch at that cafe	f. that are on display in local museums.

4 Complete the sentences with *who, that,* or *where.*

ATTENTION ALL STUDENTS!

Why is homework sometimes a problem?

- You have a little brother (1) __who/that__ is great, but (2) _____ makes a lot of noise.
- You have an older sister (3) _____ uses the computer all the time.
- You have a room (4) _____ is too small.

What's the answer

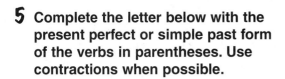

THE HOMEWORK CLUB

- We have a large room (5) _____ students can do homework.
- We have a computer room with computers (6) _____ have all the programs you need.
- There is always someone here (7) _____ can help you.
- We also have a juice bar, (8) _____ you can relax.

5 Complete the letter below with the present perfect or simple past form of the verbs in parentheses. Use contractions when possible.

July 7, _____

Dear Mom,

Thanks for the birthday presents! I especially (1. like) __liked__ the personal stereo. It's fantastic! I (2. use) _____ it a lot. I also (3. get) _____ a shirt from Grandma. How is she, by the way? (4. see) _____ you _____ her recently?

My birthday (5. be) _____ really great. I (6. have) _____ a party at the hostel on Thursday evening. The other volunteers (7. give) _____ me a Shakira CD. I (8. already / listen) _____ to the CD twice today!

We (9. be) _____ very busy recently. Our project is going well. So well, in fact, that a local TV station (10. make) _____ a program about us last week, but we (11. not / see) _____ it yet.

Lots of love,
Jan

Moving Up

6 Combine the sentences using *who, that,* or *where.*

1. I have a friend. She loves horseback riding.
   I have a friend who loves horseback riding.

2. I know a park. We can play volleyball there.
   _____

3. Water polo is a sport. It is played in a swimming pool.
   _____

4. Teenagers are people. They are between the ages of thirteen and nineteen.
   _____

5. There is a store at the beach. You can buy goggles there.
   _____

6. In-line skating is an activity. Many people love it.
   _____

7. My brother has some friends. They are great basketball players.
   _____

8. There is the electronics store. We bought our computer there.
   _____

Reaching for the Top

1 Today is Sunday. Read Carol's diary. Use her notes to write your questions and her answers. Also use the cues and the simple past and the present perfect.

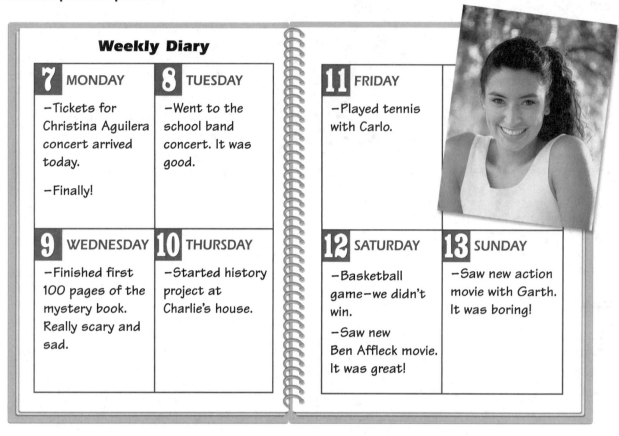

Weekly Diary

7 MONDAY
–Tickets for Christina Aguilera concert arrived today.

–Finally!

8 TUESDAY
–Went to the school band concert. It was good.

9 WEDNESDAY
–Finished first 100 pages of the mystery book. Really scary and sad.

10 THURSDAY
–Started history project at Charlie's house.

11 FRIDAY
–Played tennis with Carlo.

12 SATURDAY
–Basketball game–we didn't win.
–Saw new Ben Affleck movie. It was great!

13 SUNDAY
–Saw new action movie with Garth. It was boring!

---

1. you / see / any movies / this week
   Q: *Did you see any movies this week?*
   A: *Yes, I saw two movies—the Ben Affleck movie and an action movie.*

2. you / enjoy / the action movie
   Q: _____
   A: _____

3. you / enjoy / the Ben Affleck movie
   Q: _____
   A: _____

4. What / sports / you / play / since Friday
   Q: _____
   A: _____

5. When / play / basketball
   Q: _____
   A: _____

6. you / win / the game
   Q: _____
   A: _____

7. you / receive / tickets for the Christina Aguilera concert / yet
   Q: _____
   A: _____

8. you / go / to the school band concert / on Tuesday
   Q: _____
   A: _____

9. you / finished / the mystery book / yet
   Q: _____
   A: _____

10. you / start / the history project / yet
    Q: _____
    A: _____

Communication

Getting Started

8 Read the answers. Then complete the questions in the conversation. Use the simple past or the present perfect.

A: (1) _Have you ever been_ to China?

B: Yes, I have.

A: When (2) _____?

B: I went in March.

A: What (3) _____?

B: It was fascinating. I enjoyed it a lot.

A: Which cities
  (4) _____?

B: I visited Shanghai and Beijing, and I saw the Great Wall.

A: One of the Wonders of the World!
  _____
  any other Wonders of the World?

B: Yes, I've seen the Pyramids in Egypt.

Moving Up

9 Complete the conversation with the cues and the simple past or the present perfect. Use the conversation in Exercise 8 as a model.

(1) A: (be / Russia)

  B: (✓)

(2) A: (When / go)

  B: (go / last summer)

(3) A: (Which places / visit)

  B: (Moscow / St. Petersburg)

(4) A: (What / St. Petersburg like)

  B: (fantastic)

(5) A: (meet / any Russian students)

  B: (✓)

(6) A: (keep in touch / with any of them)

  B: (✗)

(1) A: _Have you ever been to Russia?_

  B: _Yes, I have._

(2) A: _____

  B: _____

(3) A: _____

  B: _____

(4) A: _____

  B: _____

(5) A: _____

  B: _____

(6) A: _____

  B: _____

Reaching for the Top

10 In your notebook, write a conversation in which a friend is asking you about a trip you took to another country or city. Use the conversations in Exercises 8 and 9 as models.

Friend: _Have you ever been to . . . ?_

  You: _Yes, . . ._

Study Corner

Using the Relative Pronouns *Who* and *That*

In writing and formal speech, the relative pronoun *who* is always used to refer to a person. However, in everyday conversations you may hear people use *that* instead of *who*.

FORMAL: *I know a lot of people **who** went to the concert.*

INFORMAL: *I know a lot of people **that** went to the concert.*

Reading

THE WORLD OF SHOES

People have worn hundreds of different types of shoes over the last 3,500 years. The earliest shoes were made from leaves, grass, animal skins, wood, or cloth, depending on the climate and country. People tied them around their feet to make simple sandals. From these humble beginnings, people all over the
5 world have discovered an amazing variety of ways to cover their feet.

SIMPLE SHOES In warm climates, such as in ancient Egypt, the earliest shoes were made from leaves or grass. People tied them around their feet, using vines as ties. In cold climates, people used animal skins to protect their feet. In Europe, the earliest shoes of this type were called *Opankes*, which is
10 the Siberian word for *shoe*. Opankes were made of a single piece of hide that people wrapped around their feet. Everyone made his or her own shoes.

FANCY SHOES Early shoes were called *straights*, and they would fit on either foot. By the 1700s, however, shoes were made to fit either the left foot or the right foot. In addition, shoemakers began to create a wide variety of
15 styles, some of them very fancy. Men's shoes generally had squared toes while women's shoes had pointed toes. The soles were usually made of leather.

NOISY SHOES Some early shoes were made of wood. Since they made a lot of noise, people rarely wore them inside the house. Some American
20 cowboy boots were also noisy because they had metal spurs on the heels. When a cowboy walked down the street, the spurs made a clinking sound.

QUIET SHOES For centuries, Native Americans had their own version of the *Opanke*, called the *moccasin*. Moccasins have a soft bottom, and a person wearing them makes no sound when walking. Originally,
25 moccasins were made and repaired only by women. Girls started to learn this craft when they were eight. Native Americans gave away pairs of moccasins to show their friendship, and they sometimes also traded them for food.

Another kind of quiet shoe is the sneaker. (*To sneak* means to move
30 quietly without being heard.) When an American company started making shoes with rubber instead of leather soles, the public started calling them sneakers. Today sneakers are very popular. There are hundreds of styles of sneakers: running shoes, high tops for basketball, shoes with spikes for golf, and many more.
35 What kinds of shoes and sneakers did you wear a few years ago? What kinds of shoes and sneakers do you wear now?

Vocabulary

1 Match each word with its definition. Write the letters.

_g_ 1. humble (line 4)   a. exchanged

___ 2. hide (line 10)   b. the skin of an animal

___ 3. sole (line 16)   c. the back part of the bottom of the shoe

___ 4. spur (line 20)   d. pointed pieces of metal on the sole and heel of a shoe

___ 5. heel (line 20)   e. the bottom part of the shoe

___ 6. clinking (line 21)   f. short, metallic ringing

___ 7. traded (line 27)   g. simple

___ 8. spikes (line 34)   h. pointed object worn on the heel of a rider's boot

Comprehension

2 Read the sentences. Are they true or false? Circle *T* for true or *F* for false.

1. T (F) Some of the first shoes were made of animal skins.

2. T F   A straight shoe fits either the left foot or the right foot.

3. T F   In the 1700s, most women's shoes had square toes.

4. T F   Some early shoes were made of metal.

5. T F   Some cowboy boots were noisy.

6. T F   Sneakers have rubber bottoms.

3 Number the events in the order in which they happened.

___ People started buying different kinds of sneakers for running, playing basketball, and playing golf.

___ Different shoes were made to fit the left foot and the right foot.

_1_ People made shoes from leaves, grass, animal skins, wood, or cloth.

___ Rubber was used to make the soles of shoes.

___ Women began to wear shoes with pointed toes.

Writing

4 In your notebook, write a short paragraph about your favorite kind of shoe.

Example:

I like comfortable shoes. My favorite shoes are my sandals. I can only wear them in the summer. They're made of rubber. They're red and white, and I always wear them to the beach.

9 It's the scariest ride of all!

Vocabulary

Getting Started

1 Complete the adjectives of measurement. Write the missing letters.

1. Speed   f _a_ st   s __ __ w
2. Weight   h __ __ __ y   l __ g __ t
3. Height   h __ __ __   __ __ w
4. Length   __ o __ __   __ h __ __ __
5. Duration   l __ __ __   __ __ __ __ __ t

Moving Up

2 Write the words from Exercise 1 in the puzzle. Which word does not fit? Write it on the line below.

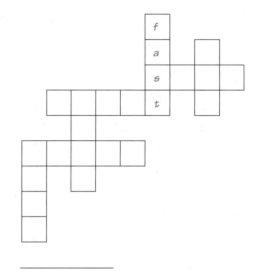

_____

Reaching for the Top

3 Look at the pictures. Then label each with an adjective of measurement.

1.
_____slow_____

2.
_____

3.
_____

4.
_____

5.
_____

6.
_____

7.
_____

8.
_____

Communication

Getting Started

4 Complete the conversations with words from the box.

~~scarier~~	high	bravest
dangerous	fast	more exciting

1.

A: Hey! Let's go snowboarding.

B: No, thanks. That's even
(1) _____scarier_____ than skiing.

A: I've never hurt myself snowboarding, and it's (2) _____ than skiing.

B: Maybe, but I'm not the
(3) _____ person around.

2.

A: How (4) _____ is this mountain?

B: Oh, about 320 feet.

A: And how (5) _____ will we go?

B: We won't ski very fast.

A: It looks a little (6) _____ to me.

B: Don't worry. You'll do fine.

Moving Up

5 Complete the conversation with sentences from the box.

> We did everything! There was so much to do.
> I went with my mom, dad, and little sister.
> ~~Yes, I did.~~
> I think the Pirates Beach was the most unforgettable. That was awesome!
> I went to EuroDisney.
> It was unbelievable!

Sandra: Did you go on a vacation last summer, Miguel?

Miguel: (1) _Yes I did._ _____

Sandra: Where did you go?

Miguel: (2) _____

Sandra: Was it fun?

Miguel: (3) _____

Sandra: Who did you go with?

Miguel: (4) _____

_____

Sandra: What did you do?

Miguel: (5) _____

_____

Sandra: What was the most unforgettable thing?

Miguel: (6) _____

_____

Reaching for the Top

6 In your notebook, write a conversation between you and a friend about a vacation you had or a trip you went on recently. Use the conversation in Exercise 5 as a model.

Grammar

Getting Started

7 Complete the chart with the missing comparative and superlative forms of the adjectives.

Positive	Comparative	Superlative
1. clean	*cleaner than*	*the cleanest*
2. fat		
3. funny		
4. exciting		
5. interesting		
6. good		
7. bad		
8. popular		
9. thin		
10. easy		

Moving Up

8 Complete the sentences with the comparative form of the adjectives in parentheses.

1. The second *Harry Potter* movie is (*good*) ___better than___ the first.

2. Geography is (*interesting*) _____ math.

3. My sister is (*short*) _____ I am.

4. Horseback riding is (*difficult*) _____ riding a bike.

5. My dad is (*young*) _____ my mom.

6. A house is (*expensive*) _____ an apartment.

7. Carlo's joke was (*funny*) _____ your joke.

8. Bungee jumping is (*exciting*) _____ sailing.

9 Rewrite the sentences from Exercise 8. Use *not as . . . as* or, where possible, *less . . . than.*

1. *The first Harry Potter movie is not as good as the second.*

2. *Math isn't as interesting as geography.* OR *Math is less interesting than geography.*

3. _____

_____

4. _____

_____

5. _____

_____

6. _____

_____

7. _____

_____

8. _____

_____

10 Read the information in the chart. Then complete the sentences. Write the comparative or superlative form of the adjectives in parentheses or *not as . . . as* and the adjective in parentheses.

	Age	Weight (Pounds)	Cost of lunch
Tiffany	13	100	$5.50
Carlo	15	125	$3.25
Billy	16	120	$5.25
Wanda	18	130	$3.75

1. (*old*) There are four children in the Baker family. Wanda is ___the oldest___. Carlo is _____ Tiffany, but _____ Billy.

2. (*heavy*) Wanda is _____. Billy is _____ Carlo, but _____ Tiffany.

3. (*expensive*) They had lunch at a restaurant today. Tiffany's lunch was _____. Wanda's lunch was _____ Billy's, but _____ Carlo's. Carlo's lunch was _____.

Reaching for the Top

11 These statements have the wrong information. Using the chart in Exercise 10, rewrite the sentences with the correct information.

1. Tiffany is older than Carlo.
   Carlo is older than Tiffany.

2. Wanda is the youngest.
   _____

3. Carlo is lighter than Billy.
   _____

4. Wanda is the lightest.
   _____

5. Billy's lunch was less expensive than Wanda's.
   _____

6. Tiffany's lunch was the cheapest.
   _____

12 Write comparisons using the cues.

1. **Britney Spears / Christina Aguilera**

   (*not as . . . as*) *Britney Spears is not as young as Christina Aguilera.*

   (*less . . . than*) _____

   (*more . . . than*) _____

2. **books / movies**

   (*not as . . . as*) _____

   (*less . . . than*) _____

   (*more . . . than*) _____

3. **bicycles / buses**

   (*not as . . . as*) _____

   (*less . . . than*) _____

   (*more . . . than*) _____

13 In your notebook, write three sentences using *as . . . as.*

Example: *The red car is as beautiful as the blue one.*

10 I was running when I fell.

Vocabulary

Getting Started

1 Look at the pictures. Then complete the action verbs.

1.

f <u>e</u> <u>l</u> <u>l</u>

2.

__ u __

3.

f __ __ __ ted

4.

b __ r __ __ d

5.

__ r __ __ hed

6.

b __ __ __ __

7.

b __ __ __ __ ed

8.

k __ __ __ e __

Moving Up

2 First, complete the puzzle clues with the correct forms of the words from Exercise 1. Then write the words in the puzzle.

Across

1. I _____ my hand while I was cooking dinner.

2. The man _____ his finger while he was fixing the TV.

5. My older brother _____ his car into the fence.

6. The soccer player _____ the ball into the goal.

7. Look! I found a baby bird. It probably _____ out of its nest.

Down

1. The ball _____ over our neighbor's fence.

3. I _____ my leg in a skiing accident last winter.

4. First, I felt lightheaded. Then I _____.

Communication

Getting Started

3 Fill in the blanks. Use the sentences from the box.

Watch out!   ~~It's not that bad.~~
It sounds like fun.   Are you all right?
It wasn't my fault.

1. _It's not that bad._

   My ankle only hurts a little.

2. _____

   That car is moving very fast!

3. I want to try skateboarding.

   _____

4. I didn't cause the accident.

   _____

5. How are you feeling?

   _____

Moving Up

4 Number the lines of the conversation in the correct order. Then write the conversation on the lines.

___ What happened?

_1_ Are you all right?

___ That's not such a good idea. I'll call the doctor.

___ I twisted my ankle.

___ I don't need one. I think I'll just lie down for a while.

___ You should probably see a doctor.

___ I don't think so.

_____

_____

_____

Reaching for the Top

5 In your notebook, write a conversation in which a friend is asking you about an accident you had. Use the conversation in Exercise 4 as a model.

Example:

Friend: _Are you OK?_

   You: _I hurt . . ._

_____

_____

_____

_____

_____

_____

Grammar

Getting Started

6 Read the paragraph in Matt's diary. Then complete the sentences. Circle *when* or *while*.

My Uncle John from Australia tried to reach me early Monday morning (1. *when* /*while*) he was getting ready to go to a business meeting, but no one answered the phone. He probably called (2. *when* / *while*) I was running in the park. I forgot to turn on the answering machine (3. *when* / *while*) I left the house. He saw my sister, Rita, (4. *when* / *while*) he was visiting San Francisco. They tried to call me (5. *when* / *while*) they were having dinner at Fisherman's Wharf, but I wasn't home. He wants to see me later in the week when he doesn't have any meetings. I saw him (6. *when* / *while*) he visited last month, but I can't wait to see him again!

7 Read the answers. Then complete the questions. Use the correct question words and *was* or *were*.

1. Q: _____What were_____ you doing when I called you last night?

   A: I was doing my homework.

2. Q: _____ dancing with Jose at the party?

   A: Julia.

3. Q: _____ the children playing when the storm started?

   A: In the yard.

4. Q: _____ you crying yesterday?

   A: Because I was unhappy.

5. Q: _____ John feeling sick?

   A: Yesterday afternoon.

6. Q: _____ Sam and Laura doing while you were cooking?

   A: They were watching TV.

Moving Up

8 Complete the sentences with the simple past or the past continuous form of the verbs in parentheses.

1. While I (*stay*) _was staying_ in Florida, I (*visit*) _visited_ an amusement park.

2. I (*get*) _____ sick while I (*ride*) _____ the roller coaster.

3. I (*be*) _____ really glad when it (*stop*) _____.

4. We (*see*) _____ a lot of tourists while we (*walk*) _____ around the park.

5. While we (*look*) _____ for a place to eat, we (*meet*) _____ our neighbors!

6. They (*stand*) _____ in line while we (*look*) _____ at the prices.

7. We (*decide*) _____ not to eat at the park when we (*see*) _____ the prices and the long lines.

9 **Rewrite the sentences using *while* or *when*.**

1. Amy was running to catch the bus when she dropped her purse.

   While Amy was running to catch the bus,

   she dropped her purse.

2. While Bobby was studying, his sister came into the room.

   _____

   _____

3. While the girls were shopping, they saw a famous movie star.

   _____

   _____

4. Alex was swimming when someone stole his wallet.

   _____

   _____

5. While Mrs. Shinsato was driving home, she saw an accident.

   _____

   _____

6. Frank and Andy were watching TV when the phone rang.

   _____

   _____

7. When Marcy arrived home, her parents were cooking dinner.

   _____

   _____

Reaching for the Top

10 **Answer the questions with true information about yourself. Use *while* or *when* in your answers.**

1. What did you learn while you were studying last night?

   While I was studying last night,

   I learned . . .

2. What happened while you were going to school today?

   _____

   _____

3. What were your classmates doing when you arrived at school today?

   _____

   _____

4. What were you thinking about while you were waiting for your class to begin?

   _____

   _____

5. What was a family member or friend doing when you arrived home from school today?

   _____

   _____

Study Corner

Using the Past Continuous

We use the past continuous to talk about ongoing events at a specific time in the past. The past continuous sometimes has two other special uses.

(1) To talk about actions that were repeated in the past:

   When Kim worked as a cook, she <u>was cutting up</u> vegetables every day.

(2) To talk about temporary situations in the past:

   Paul <u>was staying</u> home for a few days because he was sick.

11 **Read the sentences. Then write *R* for repeated actions and *T* for temporary situations.**

___ 1. I <u>was feeling</u> hungry until I ate lunch.

___ 2. When he was in Paris, Mike <u>was</u> always <u>practicing</u> his French.

___ 3. When she first came to the United States, Midori <u>was calling</u> home every night.

___ 4. Sarah <u>was resting</u> before returning to work.

11 The talk show is taped there.

Grammar

Getting Started

1 For each item, link a word or phrase from each column together to make a complete sentence. Write the sentences on the lines.

1. Most houses		shown	on computers.
2. Movies		built	in movie theaters.
3. Football	is	played	in Brazil.
4. Coffee beans	are	done	in a studio.
5. Talk shows		recorded	on a football field.
6. Special effects		grown	of wood.

1. _Most houses are built of wood._ _____

2. _____

3. _____

4. _____

5. _____

6. _____

2 Complete the sentences using the present-tense passive voice of the verbs in parentheses.

Letters (1. *collect*) _are collected_ several times a day from the mailbox. They (2. *put*) _____ into a large bag. Then they (3. *take*) _____ to the post office.

Each letter (4. *sort*) _____ by a machine. Letters going out of town (5. *place*) _____ in boxes to go to different cities. These boxes (6. *empty*) _____ into large bags. The bags (7. *send*) _____ to the other cities by truck or airplane.

When the letters arrive, they (8. *divide*) _____ into different groups—one for each neighborhood. Each mail carrier (9. *give*) _____ letters for a different neighborhood. Then the letters (10. *deliver*) _____ to different houses.

Moving Up

3 Write sentences using the passive voice in the present tense. Use the cues.

1. Many movies / make / in Hollywood
   Many movies are made in Hollywood.

2. Baseball / not / play / in this stadium

3. This movie / show / every day at 4:00 P.M.

4. Some good plays / write / by teenagers

5. Rice / not grow / in France

6. That role / play / by Gwyneth Paltrow

7. Mail / not deliver / on Sundays

8. One hundred people / employ / in this company

9. Our room / clean / every morning

10. I / not surprise / by her good grades

Reaching for the Top

4 Read the sentences about pop songs and movies. Then rewrite them using the passive voice in the present tense.

Pop Songs

1. Write the words and the music.
   The words and the music are written.

2. Choose a recording studio.

3. Record the songs.

4. Advertise the CDs.

5. Perform the songs.

Movies

6. Write the script.

7. Choose the actors.

8. Design the costumes.

9. Film the scenes.

10. Edit the movie.

Vocabulary

Getting Started

5 Look at the pictures. Then write the types of TV shows from the box under the correct pictures.

news show	documentary
talk show	~~situation comedy~~
home decorating show	game show
cooking show	cartoon

situation comedy

_____

_____

_____

_____

6.

_____

_____

_____

Moving Up

6 Complete the sentences. Use the words from Exercise 5.

1. A funny series that focuses on a situation is called a _situation comedy_ .

2. An informational program about a particular subject is called a _____.

3. A program that focuses on food and how to prepare it is a _____.

4. Contestants try to win prizes on a _____.

5. Guests are interviewed in an informal setting on a _____.

6. A program that focuses on improving the appearance of houses is a _____.

7. A program that features animated drawings, usually for children, is called a _____.

8. If you want to know what is happening in the world every day, watch a _____.

Reaching for the Top

7 On the lines below, list the shows in Exercises 5 and 6 in order of your preference. Start your list with your favorite type of show and end it with your least favorite. Then, write real examples of each type of show on your list.

Type of show	Example
1. situation comedy	Friends
2. cartoon	Scooby Doo
3.	
4.	
5.	
6.	
7.	
8.	

Communication

Getting Started

8 Complete the conversation with words from the box.

Go on.	is taped
Can you give me an example?	~~are filmed~~
That's the very idea.	You bet!
what happens	You mean

Guide: . . . And here's where some of the scenes (1) __are filmed__. Would you like to see yourself on the screen?

Allen: No, thanks.

Guide: (2) _____ Try it.

Allen: Well, OK. Wow! . . . Hey, (3) _____ when an actor forgets a line?

Guide: Each scene (4) _____ separately, so they just do the scene again.

Allen: (5) _____ they don't have to learn *all* their words at once—like in a theater play?

Guide: (6) _____

Allen: How much do the actors get paid?

Guide: Oh, they get paid quite well.

Allen: (7) _____

Guide: Some get $5,000 a day. Does that sound good to you?

Allen: (8) _____

Moving Up

9 Read the sentences. Then write answers using the passive voice in the present tense. Use the cues.

1. Do they record this TV show in New York?
   (*No / California*) _No, it's recorded_
   in California.

2. Do the writers develop all the new ideas?
   (*No / some ideas / the producers*) _____
   _____

3. Does one person write most sitcoms?
   (*No / a team of writers*) _____
   _____

4. Does the producer hire all the actors?
   (*No / some actors / the director*) _____
   _____

Study Corner

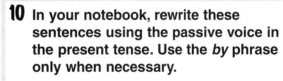

Using the Passive Voice

We use the *by* phrase in the passive voice only when it is important to know who or what performs the action. If it is not important or we do not know who performs the action, *by* is omitted.

10 In your notebook, rewrite these sentences using the passive voice in the present tense. Use the *by* phrase only when necessary.

1. Somebody steals a lot of bicycles from here.
   A lot of bicycles are stolen from here.

2. Handicapped teenagers painted the pictures in this calendar.
   The pictures in this calendar were painted by
   handicapped teenagers.

3. People make good wine in France and Spain.

4. My friend's parents own that house.

5. They serve good food in this café.

6. Mark Twain wrote *Tom Sawyer*.

12 Learning English is cool!

Grammar

Getting Started

1 Complete the conversation with the correct reflexive pronouns.

Luisa: Listen! Dad is singing to (1) _himself_ again.

Hugo: Don't laugh. He's enjoying (2) _____.

Luisa: I know. Sometimes I like to sing to (3) _____, too.

Hugo: Yes, I've heard you. You have a terrible voice. You should hear (4) _____!

Luisa: I'm not that bad! Mom's worse than I am. Do you remember that time when she recorded (5) _____?

Hugo: And played us the tape? Yes! We laughed and then got upset with (6) _____.

Luisa: I know. I felt bad. But it wasn't our fault. Our parents should learn to behave (7) _____. They act like us sometimes.

2 Complete the sentences with the gerund form of the verbs from the box.

smoke	~~take~~	get up
learn	play	exercise

1. _Taking_ vitamins is good for your health.
2. _____ in a gym keeps you in shape.
3. _____ cigarettes is unhealthy.
4. _____ soccer is a lot of fun!
5. _____ a foreign language can be difficult.
6. _____ early is hard when you're tired.

Moving Up

3 Complete the sentences. Write the correct form of a verb from the box and a reflexive pronoun.

cut	reward	~~enjoy~~	scratch
see	introduce	blame	

1. Thank you for the party. We really _enjoyed ourselves_ .

2. My mom _____ while she was cutting onions.

3. It wasn't your fault. You shouldn't _____.

4. I decided to _____ because I passed all my exams.

5. Marco walked into the studio and _____ to the director.

6. The twins laughed when they _____ in the mirror.

7. I think my dog has fleas because it can't stop _____.

4 Complete Luisa's letter. Write the gerund form of the verbs in parentheses.

Dear Mom and Dad,

I really like (1. *be*) ___being___ here at sports camp. I especially enjoy (2. *play*) _____ volleyball with my team. We're the best! My coach says that I need to practice (3. *jump*) _____ because I'm shorter than the other girls. That's okay. I don't mind (4. *train*) _____ hard if it makes me a better player.

There are many other sports here to enjoy. I'm thinking about (5. *try*) _____ squash and tennis. I can imagine (6. *be*) _____ quite good at those sports because you don't have to be tall to play them. My friend Clara is talking about (7. *play*) _____ soccer, but I don't like that sport.

Anyway, I have to stop (8. *write*) _____ now because I have volleyball practice. I'm looking forward to (9. *see*) _____ you all again next month. And Dad, I miss (10. *listen*) _____ to you sing to yourself!

Lots of love,

Luisa

Reaching for the Top

5 Read the questions. Then write answers to the questions using reflexive pronouns. Use the cues.

1. Who helped you do your homework?
   No one. I _____ *did it myself* _____.

2. Did a mechanic repair Sally's car?
   No, she _____.

3. Would you like me to carry your bags?
   No, thanks. I'll _____.

4. Did John's mother clean his room for him?
   No way! He _____.

5. Who paid for Mark's and Simon's dinners?
   Nobody. They _____.

6. Make me a sandwich.
   No! _____!

6 Rewrite the sentences using gerunds as subjects.

1. It feels good to sleep in my own bed again.
   Sleeping in my own bed again feels good.

2. It's wrong to steal things.
   _____

3. It's expensive to live in New York.
   _____

4. It's easy to make Susan laugh.
   _____

5. It's fun to chat with friends on the Internet.
   _____

6. It takes years to learn a foreign language.
   _____

7. It's dangerous to drive too fast.
   _____

Vocabulary

Getting Started

7 Look at the pictures. Then complete the name of each extracurricular activity. Write the missing letters.

1.

   s <u>c</u> <u>i</u> <u>e</u> <u>n</u> <u>c</u> <u>e</u> c <u>l</u> <u>u</u> <u>b</u>

2.

   s _ _ _ _ l b _ _ _

3.

   d _ _ _ a c _ _ _ _

4.

   c _ _ _ _ _ _ _ r c _ _ _ _

5.

   a _ _ c _ _ _

6.

   y _ _ _ _ _ _ k

Moving Up

8 Read these advertisements. Then write the name of the club each ad is for.

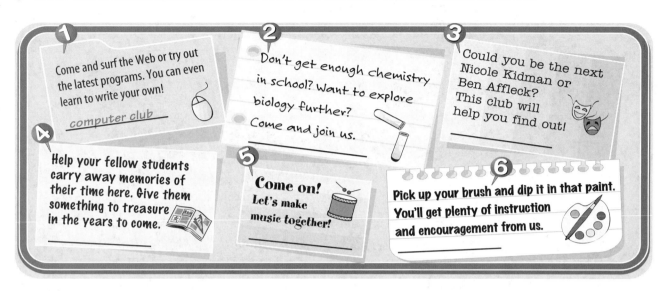

1. Come and surf the Web or try out the latest programs. You can even learn to write your own!
   computer club

2. Don't get enough chemistry in school? Want to explore biology further? Come and join us.

3. Could you be the next Nicole Kidman or Ben Affleck? This club will help you find out!

4. Help your fellow students carry away memories of their time here. Give them something to treasure in the years to come.

5. Come on! Let's make music together!

6. Pick up your brush and dip it in that paint. You'll get plenty of instruction and encouragement from us.

Reaching for the Top

9 Choose an extracurricular club or activity from Exercises 7 and 8 or make up your own. In your notebook, write an advertisement for the club encouraging people to join. Use the advertisements in Exercise 8 as models.

Communication

Moving Up

10 Complete the conversation with words from the box.

> I'd like to keep on going to that
> ~~Are you joining any clubs this year?~~
> I enjoy acting
> couldn't stand learning all those lines
> avoid working after school hours
> are you considering joining

Tony: Hey, Kim. (1) _Are you joining any clubs this year?_

Kim: Yes, I think so. One or two.

Tony: What clubs (2) _____?

Kim: Well, (3) _____.
So I might join the drama club.

Tony: Ugh! I tried acting once. I
(4) _____!

Kim: Hmm. I wouldn't mind that.

Tony: What other clubs are you thinking about joining?

Kim: Well, I was in the Language Club last year. I studied Spanish. So
(5) _____.

Tony: The Language Club sounds like a lot of work! I always try to
(6) _____!

Kim: Yes, Tony. I know. So, are you going to join any clubs this year?

Tony: I'm not planning to. But I can't help thinking that I'll be missing out on something.

Kim: You will be!

Reaching for the Top

11 In your notebook, write a conversation between you and a friend about what clubs you are going to join or are not going to join at the beginning of the school year. Use the conversation in Exercise 10 as a model.

Reading

I can do that!

Each year, Hollywood produces more and more action movies. These movies have scenes showing people in really dangerous situations. They jump from tall buildings, crash cars, get into fights, and run through
5 burning houses. Since most actors aren't willing to put themselves in any danger—or their insurance companies aren't willing to let them—other people are used when these scenes are filmed.

People who perform this kind of work are called stunt
10 doubles. (A *stunt* is a difficult trick; a *double* is a person who looks very similar to someone else.) All famous actors have stunt doubles. The stunt double is usually the same age and size as the actor. Sometimes, however, the stunt double has to wear a wig and makeup in order to
15 look more like the actor.

Stunt doubles make a lot of money but not nearly as much as as actors do. An experienced stunt double who works regularly can earn $100,000 a year or more. But a well-known actor can make millions. Stunt doubles don't
20 work all the time. They are paid to do certain scenes in a movie, and then they aren't needed anymore for that movie. As a result, they are constantly looking for work.

The job has a strange mix of advantages and disadvantages. Stunt work is great for people who like to
25 be outdoors. Stunt doubles meet many famous people, and the job provides free travel to the interesting and scenic places where the movies are made. However, stunt doubles are often away from home and family. Stunt doubles work long and hard. Sometimes they get up as
30 early as 4 A.M., and their day can last fourteen hours. And a stunt double's career is usually over by the age of forty. At that point, the person's body is ready for retirement!

Vocabulary

1 Match each word with its definition. Write the letters.

__e__ 1. willing (line 5)   a. steadily

____ 2. regularly (line 18)   b. with beautiful views

____ 3. constantly (line 22)   c. that period of time after a person stops working

____ 4. advantage (line 23)   d. something that helps a person to be (successful, happy, etc.)

____ 5. disadvantage (line 24)   e. eager

____ 6. scenic (line 27)   f. something that *doesn't* help a person to be (successful, happy, etc)

____ 7. retirement (line 32)   g. often

Comprehension

2 Complete the sentences with words from the box. Write true sentences based on the reading. Use capital letters when necessary.

~~actors~~ retire travel indoors money insurance companies

1. Stunt doubles must look like the ____actors____ they are replacing.

2. _____ don't allow actors to perform certain stunts.

3. Stunt doubles make less _____ than actors.

4. Most stunt doubles _____ at the age of forty.

5. Stunt work is a good career choice for people who like to _____.

6. Stunt work is usually not done _____.

3 Read the text again. In the chart, write three advantages and three disadvantages of stunt work.

Advantages	Disadvantages
1. *Stunt people travel free to interesting and scenic places.*	1. _____
2. _____	2. _____
3. _____	3. _____

Writing

4 Think of a job you might like to have someday. In your notebook, write a short paragraph about the advantages and disadvantages of this job.

Example:

Being a veterinarian would be an interesting job. I love animals, and I would get to work with them every day. However, I would have to study many years. I would also have to work long hours.

Grammar Builder

Unit 1

Grammar Highlights

The simple present contrasted with the present continuous

Simple present

I usually **walk** to school.

He ⎫
She ⎭ usually **walks** to school.

You ⎫
We ⎬ usually **walk** to school at 8:00.
They ⎭

Present continuous

I**'m walking** to school right now.

He**'s** ⎫
She**'s** ⎭ **walking** to school right now.

You**'re** ⎫
We**'re** ⎬ **walking** to school right now.
They**'re** ⎭

> **Remember:** Use the simple present tense to describe a habitual action. Use the present continuous to describe an activity that is happening right now.

Position of adverbs of frequency

With *be*

Martin is {
always
usually
often
sometimes amusing.
rarely
never
}

How often is Martin rude?
How often does Sara forget her purse?
How often do you beat Tom at chess?

With other verbs

Sara {
always
usually
often
sometimes forgets things.
rarely
never
}

He is **never** rude.
She **often** forgets her purse.
I **always** beat Tom at chess.

> **Remember:**
> • Adverbs of frequency answer the question "How often?"
> • Adverbs of frequency come **after** the verb *be*, but **before** a main verb.
> • Some frequency adverbs (*sometimes, usually, often*) can come at the beginning of a sentence.
> **Usually**, I don't like horror movies.

Practice

The simple present contrasted with the present continuous

1 Complete the sentences by circling the letter next to the correct answer.

1. I always _____ my breakfast at the bus stop.

   (a.) eat   b. am eating   c. eats

2. He _____ sugar in his coffee.

   a. isn't usually taking   b. doesn't usually
   c. usually isn't taking   take

3. _____ to this music, or can I turn it off?

   a. Do you listen
   b. Does he listen   c. Are you listening

4. _____ any famous people?

   a. Are you knowing   b. You know
   c. Do you know

5. My sister _____ with a friend in California at the moment.

   a. is staying   b. stays   c. doesn't stay

6. We sometimes _____ in the woods near my house.

   a. camping   b. are camping   c. camp

7. _____ always work at the pool on Saturday evenings?

   a. Do they   b. Are they   c. Is he

8. I'm busy right now. I _____ a cake for Eddie's birthday.

   a. make   b. 'm making   c. do make

9. _____ the last time we went on vacation?

   a. Do you remember   b. Remember you
   c. Are you remembering

10. I can't go out tonight because I _____ a cold.

    a. have   b. 'm having   c. am have

2 Rewrite the sentences using the cues. Write the simple present or the present continuous form of the verbs in parentheses.

1. Andrea (*help*) her dad with the barbecue right now.

   Andrea's helping her dad with the barbecue

   right now.

2. Can I turn off the TV? I (*try*) to read my book.

   _____

3. (*you / have*) Pedro's address? I (*not / know*) where he lives.

   _____

4. You can have my cheese sandwich if you want. I (*not / like*) it.

   _____

5. Clara (*have*) a great time at her cousins' house right now.

   _____

6. What time (*you / usually / arrive*) at school in the morning?

   _____

7. It (*not / rain*) much here in the summer, but it (*rain*) now!

   _____

8. Listen! My sister (*sing*). She (*have*) a great voice.

   _____

Practice

3 Complete the letter using the cues. Write the simple present or present continuous form of the verbs in parentheses. Use contractions when possible.

Dear Tara,

I (1. *have*) _'m having_ a fantastic time in Florida. I (2. *stay*) _____ with my aunt and uncle and two cousins. I (3. *have*) _____ a long list of books to read before school starts again, but I (4. *not / read*) _____ any of them! In fact, I (5. *not / use*) _____ my brain at all! Instead I (6. *get*) _____ a suntan! Right now I (7. *sit*) _____ on the edge of the swimming pool with my feet in the water. I (8. *sip*) _____ a big chocolate milkshake.

Every day we (9. *go*) _____ to the beach. I (10. *learn how*) _____ to water ski! I'm not very good yet and I often (11. *fall down*) _____, but it's fun. Sometimes, I (12. *play*) _____ volleyball with my cousins, their friends, and other people on the beach. I often (13. *not / hit*) _____ the ball over the net, but I still (14. *have*) _____ lots of fun!

The food is great. I usually (15. *have*) _____ fresh-squeezed orange juice and cereal for breakfast. We (16. *not / eat*) _____ a big lunch—usually just sandwiches and fruit salad. In the evenings, my uncle always (17. *cook*) _____ on the grill. I (18. *love*) _____ that!

(19. *you / have*) _____ a nice time in California? Is your job at the pizza restaurant okay? What time (20. *you / start*) _____ work every day? (21. *they / give*) _____ you a free meal while you're there?

Write soon and tell me all your news.

Love, Carla

Position of adverbs of frequency

4 Read the questions. Then complete the answers. Circle the appropriate adverb of frequency.

1. Q: Does Gloria read magazines in English?

   A: She (often / never) reads an English magazine. She buys one every morning.

2. Q: Does Marco sing in English?

   A: He (often / rarely) sings. He doesn't like to sing.

3. Q: Do you go out with your friends on weekends?

   A: I (never / always) go out on weekends. I work on Saturdays and Sundays.

4. Q: Do the students in your class practice English at home?

   A: They like English. They (usually / never) practice English in the evenings.

5. Q: Does Tetsuo write e-mails in Japanese?

   A: His family is in Japan. He misses them very much. He (always / rarely) writes e-mails to them in Japanese.

6. Q: Does Anna practice swimming a lot?

   A: She (sometimes / always) practices at the school pool. She's there about twice a week.

Practice

5 Unscramble the words to write sentences. Be sure to put the adverbs of frequency in the correct place.

1. my / Saturday / evenings / with / On / usually / hang out / I / friends

   On Saturday evenings I usually hang out with
   my friends.

2. rarely / school bus / is / late / Our

   _____

3. in / baseball games / watch / never / the park / We

   _____

4. tired / I'm / in / evening / always / the

   _____

5. after / video games / play / we / school / Sometimes

   _____

6. We / eat / dinner / usually / at 6:00 P.M.

   _____

7. forgets / always / Jack / his bed / make / to

   _____

8. the school year / go / rarely / on vacation / They / during

   _____

9. teacher / tells / jokes / funny / Our / never

   _____

10. is / late / Sandra / for school / usually

    _____

6 Write questions and answers about how often Gino does the activities listed in the chart.

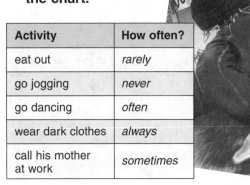

Activity	How often?
eat out	*rarely*
go jogging	*never*
go dancing	*often*
wear dark clothes	*always*
call his mother at work	*sometimes*

1. *How often does Gino eat out?*
   He rarely eats out.

2. _____
   _____

3. _____
   _____

4. _____
   _____

5. _____
   _____

7 Answer the questions with true information about yourself. Use an adverb of frequency in your answers.

1. How often do you go rock climbing?
   I never go rock climbing.

2. How often do you exercise?

   _____

3. How often do you dream in English?

   _____

4. How often do you listen to opera?

   _____

5. How often do you wash the dishes at home?

   _____

6. How often do you think about food?

   _____

Grammar Highlights

The simple past tense: regular verbs

Affirmative statements

Simon **walked** to work.
She **stayed** with her aunt.

Negative statements

Simon **did not (didn't) walk** to work.
She **did not (didn't) stay** with her cousin.

***Yes/No* questions**

Did she **stay** with her aunt?

Short answers

Yes, she **did**. / No, she **didn't**.

Information questions

Where **did** you **work** last year?
What time **did** the movie **start**?

Short answers

In a restaurant.
At 7:35.

> **Remember:** The spellings of some verbs change when you add *-d* or *-ed*.
> hurry = hurr**ied**   stop = stop**ped**

The simple past tense: irregular verbs

Affirmative statements

She **spent** the day at the beach.
We **saw** an accident last night.
I **took** a shower this morning.

Negative statements

She **didn't spend** the day at the beach.
We **didn't see** an accident last night.
I **didn't take** a shower this morning.

***Yes/No* questions**

Did she **spend** the day at the beach?

Short answers

Yes, she **did**. / No, she **didn't**.

Information questions

What did you **eat** this morning?
How did she **get** to the party?

Short answers

I **ate** an egg.
She **drove**.

> **Remember:** Learn the simple past forms of irregular verbs by heart.

Practice

The simple past tense: regular verbs

1 Complete the sentences with the simple past tense of the verbs in parentheses.

1. Harry (*call*) __called__ Sharon at midnight last night.
2. We (*stop*) _____ at the store on the way home.
3. They (*hurry*) _____ home after the rock concert.
4. I (*visit*) _____ my grandparents last week.
5. When we were kids, we (*live*) _____ in Mexico.
6. Mario (*cook*) _____ dinner for his family.
7. I (*like*) _____ the new Harry Potter movie.
8. She (*enjoy*) _____ her trip to Portugal.
9. Tina (*cry*) _____ a lot when she watched the movie.
10. He (*play*) _____ with his dog after school.
11. It (*rain*) _____ all afternoon.
12. Cristina (*jog*) _____ in her new sneakers.

2 Change the sentences in Exercise 1 into negative statements. Use contractions when possible.

1. *Harry didn't call Sharon at midnight last night.*
2. _____
3. _____
4. _____
5. _____
6. _____
7. _____
8. _____
9. _____
10. _____
11. _____
12. _____

Practice

The simple past tense: irregular verbs

3 Complete the sentences with the simple past tense of the verbs from the box.

eat	go	~~have~~	leave	see
fall	grow	keep	lose	take

1. I hope you __had__ a good time at the party last night.

2. We _____ some great photos on vacation last summer.

3. Jake _____ this movie when he was eleven years old.

4. I _____ too much chocolate. I don't feel good.

5. Unfortunately, she _____ the game.

6. The teacher _____ our books in the closet.

7. Sam _____ and broke his leg when he was skiing yesterday.

8. The train _____ at noon.

9. We _____ to the new dance club last night.

10. We _____ many kinds of flowers in our garden last year.

4 Complete the sentences. Write the affirmative or the negative form of the verbs.

1. Yuri _didn't make_ a cake. He made some cookies.

2. The show didn't begin at 7:00. It _began_ at 8:00.

3. Noriko _____ a bath. She took a shower.

4. Mom and Dad _____ to Mexico on vacation. They flew to Brazil.

5. You didn't lose your ticket to the concert. You _____ my ticket.

6. He _____ a letter. He sent an e-mail.

7. The teacher didn't tell us a story. He _____ us a joke.

8. Mom didn't give me five dollars. She _____ me ten dollars.

9. Sam _____ a video game. He bought some CDs.

10. I didn't hurt my leg in the accident. I _____ my arm.

5 Read the answers. Then write information questions. Use the underlined words as cues.

1. Q: _When did you wake up today?_

   A: I woke up at 6 A.M. this morning.

2. Q: _____

   A: Molly cried because her boyfriend broke up with her.

3. Q: _____

   A: Mom and Dad saw a play yesterday.

4. Q: _____

   A: The children slept all afternoon.

5. Q: _____

   A: Rico went cycling in the park.

6. Q: _____

   A: Jose and Tran ate breakfast at 10 A.M.

7. Q: _____

   A: Kevin got to the party by subway.

Practice

6 Complete the article using the cues. Write the simple past form
of the verbs in parentheses.

Sandra Bullock – Portrait of a Star

Sandra (1. *live*) ___lived___ in Austria until she was twelve years old. She was a good student, and (2. *get*) _____ A's in all her school subjects. When her family (3. *move*) _____ to the United States and she (4. *go*) _____ to junior high school, she (5. *find*) _____ it hard to make friends. The other students (6. *not / like*) _____ her because she was very smart and because she was from another country.

So she (7. *decide*) _____ to be "ordinary." She (8. *not / do*) _____ her homework. She (9. *stop*) _____ taking drama classes. She (10. *buy*) _____ the same clothes as the other students. Suddenly, she (11. *have*) _____ lots of friends. In college, she (12. *study*) _____ drama and (13. *start*) _____ to appear in movies. Her first movies weren't very successful, but then she (14. *get*) _____ a part in *Speed* with Keanu Reeves. She is very popular now and earns more than $10 million per movie!

7 Complete the journalist's questions and Sandra's answers
with information from Exercise 6. Use the cues.

1. Q: (*you / live*) ___Did you live___ in the United
States when you were young?
   A: ___No, I didn't. I lived in Austria.___

2. Q: (*you / get*) _____ good grades
at school in Austria?
   A: _____

3. Q: (*you / have*) _____ any
problems after you moved to the United
States?
   A: _____

4. Q: What (*you / decide*) _____ to
do?
   A: _____

5. Q: (*you / study*) _____ science in
college?
   A: _____

6. Q: When (*you / become*) _____
successful in the movies?
   A: _____

Unit 3

Grammar Highlights

Have to: simple present

Affirmative statements

I/You/We/They **have to** wash the car.
He/She **has to** study after school.

Yes/No questions

Do you **have to get up** early?
Does he **have to walk** the dog?

> **Remember:** *Has to* and *have to*
> express necessity and obligation.

Negative statements

I/You/We/They **don't have to** make the bed.
He/She **doesn't have to** wear a uniform.

Short answers

Yes, I **do**. / No, I **don't**.
Yes, he **does**. / No, he **doesn't**.

Have to: simple past

Affirmative statements

I **had to do** my homework last night.
She **had to buy** a new dress.

Yes/No questions

Did you **have to** get a taxi?

Information questions

Where **did** she **have to** go?
Why **did** Jim **have to** stay up late?

> **Remember:** *Had to* is the simple
> past form of *have to.*

Negative statements

We **didn't have to** go to school yesterday.
He **didn't have to** pay for his meal.

Short answers

Yes, I **did**. / No, I **didn't**.

Answers

She **had to go** home.
Because he **had to study** for a test.

Practice

Have to: simple present

1 Complete the sentences with *has to, have to, doesn't have to,* or *don't have to*.

1. A bus driver

a. She ___has to___ have a driver's license.

b. She _____ use a computer.

c. She _____ drive safely.

2. A flight attendant

a. He _____ wear a uniform.

b. He _____ be very polite.

c. He _____ pay for plane tickets.

3. Professional basketball players

a. They _____ work in an office every day.

b. They _____ train hard.

c. They _____ wear hard hats.

2 Complete Juan's letter with *have to, has to, don't have to,* or *doesn't have to*.

February 12, _____

Dear Suki,

Hi. What's new?

I have a Saturday job working in a restaurant. I ___have to___ work quite late—until 10:00 P.M. I don't
(1)

mind working late because I _____ get up early. I only _____ be at work by 2:00 P.M. I
(2)   (3)

_____ wear a uniform, but that's OK. It's a black T-shirt that says "The Hungry Horse." I'm a kitchen
(4)

assistant—that means I _____ help in the kitchen. I'm not a chef, so I _____ do any real
(5)   (6)

cooking. But the chef _____ make salads. That's my job! When I arrive, I usually _____ wash
(7)   (8)

the vegetables and cut them up. Then I _____ make the salads. I also _____ wash the dishes
(9)   (10)

and clean the floor. But I _____ serve the food or clear the tables. The waiters, Bill and Julio,
(11)

_____ do that.
(12)

One problem is my homework. I can't do any of it on Saturday because of this job. So I _____ do
(13)

it all on Sunday.

See you soon.

Your friend,
Juan

Practice

3 **Complete the questions. Use *have to* and a verb from the box. (Some verbs can be used more than once.) Then write true answers about yourself.**

ask	clean	get up	wear
be	do	study	

1. What chores <u>*do you have to do*</u> at home?
   <u>*I have to wash the dishes every night.*</u>

2. <u>*Do you have to ask*</u> your parents before you can go to a party?
   <u>*Yes, I do.* OR *No, I don't.*</u>

3. What time _____ home?
   _____

4. How many hours of homework _____ every day?
   _____

5. How often _____ your room?
   _____

6. What time _____ in the morning?
   _____

7. What time _____ at school?
   _____

8. _____ a school uniform?
   _____

9. In your school, _____ a foreign language?
   _____

Have to: simple past

4 **Complete the sentences with *had to* or *didn't have to*.**

Lola tried to get a part on a TV commercial last week. She <u>*had to*</u> say "Splash is my
(1)
favorite perfume." She also _____ smile a
(2)
lot. But she was happy because she _____
(3)

wear any Splash perfume. She doesn't like it! It's really strong.

Paulo, Lola's boyfriend, _____ take a
(4)
Spanish exam last week. He _____ read a
(5)
passage and then answer questions about it. But he _____ do any writing because it
(6)
was an oral exam. He _____ do the
(7)
written part of the exam yesterday.

5 **Read the sentences. Then write questions using the cues.**

1. Tom had to go to the hospital last week.
   Why <u>*did Tom have to go to the hospital*</u> ?

2. I had to get up early this morning.
   What time _____ ?

3. We had to wait for the bus to arrive.
   How long _____ ?

4. My father had to stay late at work yesterday.
   Why _____ ?

5. I had to pay a lot of money for this ticket.
   How much _____ ?

6. Gail and I had to go out last night.
   Where _____ ?

7. Our class had to organize a debate.
   What _____ ?

Practice

6 Linda is a waitress, and Hiro is a chef at a restaurant. Look at the chart. What did they have to do last night? What didn't they have to do? Write six sentences using *had to* or *didn't have to*.

Things to do	Linda	Hiro
1. Cook the food	X	✓
2. Take food orders	✓	X
3. Clean the floor	X	X
4. Wear a uniform	✓	✓
5. Greet the customers	✓	X
6. Wash the dishes	✓	X
7. Get to work on time	✓	✓
8. Clear the tables	✓	X

1. *Linda didn't have to cook the food.*
2. *Hiro had to cook the food.*
3. *Linda and Hiro didn't have to clean the floor.*
4. _____
5. _____
6. _____
7. _____
8. _____
9. _____

7 What did you have to do when you were six years old? What *didn't* you have to do? What do you have to do now? What *don't* you have to do now? Write a brief paragraph using the present and past forms of *have to*.

When I was six years old, I had to go to bed at 8 P.M., and I didn't have to do homework. Now I don't

have to go to bed until 11 P.M., but I have to do homework every night.

_____
_____
_____
_____
_____

Grammar Highlights

The present continuous to express future time

Affirmative statements

I **am going** to the match tomorrow.
You **are meeting** Simon later.

Yes/No questions

Are you **going** to the match tomorrow?
Is Marco **coming** tonight?

Information questions

Where **are** they **going** tomorrow?
What **are** you **doing** tonight?

Negative statements

I **am not going** to the library tomorrow.
You **are not meeting** Martin later.

Short answers

Yes, I **am**. / No, I'm **not**.
Yes, he **is**. / No, he **isn't**.

Answers

They**'re going** to the beach.
I**'m doing** my homework.

> **Remember:** Use the present continuous to express future plans that are definite.

Verb + infinitive

I **want to see** the new *Lord of the Rings* movie.
They **promised to drive** me home.

> **Remember:** The following verbs can be followed by an infinitive.
>
> | | | | | | |
> |---|---|---|---|---|---|
> | can't afford | fail | learn | plan | try | would like |
> | agree | forget | need | promise | can't wait | would prefer |
> | decide | hope | offer | refuse | want | |

The present continuous to express future time

1 Complete the sentences. Use the present continuous for the future in affirmative and negative forms. Use contractions when possible.

1. I went to the gym yesterday, and ___I'm going___ to the gym again today.

2. Stacy didn't stay home last night, and _____ home tonight either.

3. We visited our grandparents last week, and _____ them again next week.

4. They didn't spend last night in a hotel, and _____ tonight in a hotel either.

5. You played on the soccer team last year, and _____ this year, too.

6. I got up early this morning, and _____ early tomorrow morning, too.

7. He didn't leave work at 5:00 P.M. yesterday, and _____ work at 5:00 P.M. today.

8. She didn't take the bus home last week, and _____ the bus home this week either.

2 Read the sentences about what three couples are doing on different days this weekend. Then complete the sentences using the cues and the present continuous for the future in affirmative and negative forms.

Luisa is watching videos at home on Friday night.

Ned is going over to Luisa's house on Friday night.

Marco is playing tennis on Sunday afternoon.

Cathy is meeting Marco on Sunday afternoon.

Anita is going to an 'NSync concert on Saturday night.

Frankie is going to an 'NSync concert on Saturday night.

1. On ___Friday___ night, Ned and Luisa ___are watching___ videos.

2. Ned ___is not watching___ videos on Saturday night.

3. Marco _____ tennis with _____ on Sunday afternoon.

4. Cathy and Luisa _____ to a concert on Sunday afternoon.

5. Frankie _____ to an 'NSync concert with _____ on Saturday night.

6. On Saturday night, Anita _____ videos with Ned.

7. Luisa and Marco _____ tennis on Saturday night.

Practice

3 Complete the conversation. Write
questions using the cues and
the present continuous for the future.

Yoko: I'm going on vacation this winter.

Ken: Really? (1) (*where / go*)
<u>Where are you going</u> ?

Yoko: I'm going to Colorado.

Ken: (2) (*who / go / with*)
_____ ?

Yoko: My girlfriend and her brother.

Ken: (3) (*how long / stay*)
_____ ?

Yoko: Two weeks.

Ken: (4) (*go / skiing*)
_____ ?

Yoko: Yes, we are.

Ken: (5) (*where / stay*)
_____ ?

Yoko: In a five-star hotel!

Ken: (6) (*how / get there*)
_____ ?

Yoko: We're flying to Denver. Then we're
renting a car.

Ken: (7) (*you / drive*)
_____ ?

Yoko: No, I'm not. I don't have a license. My
girlfriend's brother is driving.

4 Look at Martina's diary. Then complete
the conversation.

> **Monday:**
> *Movies with Mario 4 P.M. – 7 P.M.*
>
> **Tuesday:**
> *Watch basketball game 7 P.M. – 10 P.M.*
>
> **Wednesday:**
> *Meet some friends for dinner*
> *6 P.M. – 10 P.M.*
>
> **Thursday:**
> *Go to gym 6 P.M. – 8 P.M.*
>
> **Friday:**
> *Visit grandparents 5 P.M. – 11 P.M.*
>
> **Saturday:**
> *Rock concert with Gino*
> *8 P.M. – midnight*

Gino: Do you want to go out with me
sometime this week?

Martina: Sure, what day?

Gino: Are you doing anything on Monday
evening?

Martina: Yes, I am. (1) <u>I'm going to the</u>
<u>movies with Mario.</u>

Gino: Oh. Can you go out with me on
Tuesday evening?

Martina: No, sorry. (2) _____

Gino: What about Wednesday?

Martina: (3) _____

Gino: Thursday?

Martina: (4) _____

Gino: What about Friday? Can you go out
with me then?

Martina: Sorry. (5) _____

Gino: Wow. I bet you're doing something
on Saturday, too, aren't you?

Martina: Yes, I am. (6) _____

Gino: Oh, yes! I forgot about that!

Practice

5 Write sentences with true information about yourself. Use the present continuous for the future in affirmative or negative forms and the cues in parentheses.

1. (*next summer*)

   Next summer, I'm going to the United

   States. OR *Next summer, I'm not going to*

   summer school.

2. (*this weekend*)

   _____

3. (*this evening*)

   _____

4. (*tomorrow morning*)

   _____

5. (*next Christmas*)

   _____

Verb + infinitive

6 Complete the sentences with the verbs from the box.

buy	help	practice	sleep
eat	lock	~~rain~~	spend
go	play	see	write

1. It began _to rain_ while I was walking home last night.

2. Miguel promised _____ to me, but I haven't received one letter from him yet.

3. I forgot _____ my car doors, and someone stole my purse from the front seat.

4. They can't afford _____ so much money on a new house!

5. She got upset when I refused _____ her with homework.

6. Nora is planning _____ to Spain next year.

7. You're a good volleyball player, but you need _____ more.

8. Mrs. Collins agreed _____ her son a new bike.

9. He's learning how _____ the guitar.

10. You look tired. Why don't you lie down and try _____.

11. The baby is hungry. She needs _____ her dinner now.

12. It's been a long time. I can't wait _____ you!

7 Imagine you are going on vacation. Complete the sentences with your own ideas. Use infinitives.

1. I decided to _____ *go to Hawaii* _____.
2. I'm planning _____.
3. I hope _____.
4. I would like _____.
5. I would prefer _____.
6. I will try _____.
7. I want _____.
8. I can't wait _____.
9. I'm planning _____.

Unit 5

Grammar Highlights

Will and *won't* for decisions and promises

Affirmative statements

I**'ll have** ice cream.
Your order **will be** ready soon.

Negative statements

I **won't have** pudding.
His order **won't be** ready soon.

Will and *won't* for future predictions

Yes/No questions

Will the order **be** ready soon?
Will you **meet** me at the diner?

Short answers

Yes, it **will**. / No, it **won't**.
Yes, I **will**. / No, I **won't**.

Information questions

When **will** they **buy** the tickets?
Where **will** they **be** at 4 P.M.?

Short answers

At 2 P.M.
At Marcia's house.

The imperative

Affirmative statements

Sit down.
Please **open** the window.
Turn left here.

Negative statements

Don't sit down.
Please **don't open** the window.
Don't turn left here.

> **Remember:** Use the imperative to give a command, make a polite request, and give directions.
> The base form of the verb is used in the imperative. The negative form is formed from *don't* + the base form of the verb.

Practice

Will and *won't* for decisions and promises

1 Complete the dialogue with the correct forms of *will* + *have* or *won't* + *have*. Use contractions when possible.

Server: Hello. Are you ready to order?

Allison: I think so. . . . I'm really hungry.

I *'ll have* _____ a chicken noodle
<u>(1)</u>

soup, a mixed green salad, and the

grilled chicken.

Travis: I'm really hungry, but I _____
<u>(2)</u>

any soup. I _____ a mixed
<u>(3)</u>

green salad and a seafood platter.

My brother _____ any soup
<u>(4)</u>

either. He loves pasta, so he

_____ the pasta special.
<u>(5)</u>

Server: OK, thank you. I'll be back shortly

with your orders.

Will and *won't* for future predictions

2 Unscramble the words to write *Yes/No* questions.

1. you / on Saturday night / Will / be / at the 'NSync concert

   Will you be at the 'NSync concert on Saturday

   night?

2. that backpack / your mom / buy / you / Will

   _____

   _____

3. try out / Will / for the school band / they

   _____

   _____

4. next Friday night / sing / she / Will / at your party

   _____

   _____

5. play / Will / at our next concert / the piano / I

   _____

   _____

6. be / home / before 6 P.M. / we / Will

   _____

   _____

7. Will / on July 7 / you / to the dance / invite / he

   _____

   _____

Practice

3 Write five *Yes/No* questions and short answers. Use the cues.

1. ride your bike / after school

   <u>Will you ride your bike after school?</u>

   No, <u>I won't</u>   .

2. finish her report / before next Monday

   _____

   Yes, _____ .

3. wash his dad's car / after lunch

   _____

   No, _____ .

4. walk their dogs together / tomorrow morning

   _____

   Yes, _____ .

5. buy our lunches / at school / tomorrow

   _____

   No, _____ .

4 Look at the invitation below for Suki's birthday party. Write information questions and answers about the invitation. Use the cues.

You are invited to a birthday party!

For: Suki Hirano
Place: Marco's Bowling Alley
Date: Saturday, February 11
Time: 1—4 P.M.
We'll have pizza, soda, and cake!
Please call: 631-555-0628
I hope you'll come!

1. Where

   <u>Where will the party be?</u>   <u>It will be at Marco's Bowling Alley.</u>

2. When

   _____   _____

3. What time / start

   _____   _____

4. What time / end

   _____   _____

5. What food and drinks / serve

   _____   _____

5 Write five information questions and answers about a future school event. Use the cues.

1. What

   <u>What will the event be?</u>

   <u>It will be . . .</u>

2. When

   _____

   _____

3. Where

   _____

   _____

4. What time / start

   _____

   _____

5. What time / end

   _____

   _____

Practice

The imperative

6 Match the situations with the imperatives. Write the letters.

___c___ 1. You are watching a movie in a theater. Two people in front of you are talking loudly. What do you say?

_____ 2. You are a passenger in a car. The driver is going too fast. What do you shout?

_____ 3. A man hears someone knock on his door. What does he say?

_____ 4. In a hospital, a nurse sees a visitor smoking. What does she say?

_____ 5. A truck is driving down the street. A man starts to cross the street. What do you shout?

_____ 6. A man falls into a river. He can't swim. What does he shout?

_____ 7. A museum guard sees a little boy put his hand on an expensive piece of art. What does she say?

a. Watch out!

b. Help me!

c. Please be quiet.

d. Slow down!

e. Please don't touch the painting.

f. Please come in!

g. Please don't smoke in here.

7 Complete the imperatives. Write the affirmative or negative form of the verbs in the box. One verb is used two times.

eat	leave	lock	put	show	stop	take	wear

Zest Health Club Rules

___Show___ your membership card at the reception desk.

___Don't leave___ money in your locker.

_____ your locker.

_____ street shoes in the pool area.

_____ comfortable clothes when you exercise.

_____ food in the health club.

_____ exercising if you feel dizzy.

_____ any equipment out of the health club.

_____ the weights back in their box when you're done exercising.

Grammar Highlights

Adjectives and adverbs of manner

Adjectives	Adverbs	Examples
quiet	quietly	Tom is **quiet**. / He speaks **quietly**.
careful	carefully	I am a **careful** worker. / I work **carefully**.
happy	happily	The children are **happy**. / They are playing **happily**.
fast	fast	She is a **fast** driver. / She drives **fast**.
hard	hard	This homework was **hard**. / We worked **hard** to finish it.
early	early	The train is **early**. / It arrived **early**.
late	late	The bus is **late**. / It arrived **late**.
good	well	He is a **good** singer. / He sings **well**.

Remember: An adjective describes a noun.
- I am a **careful** worker.

An adverb gives more information about a verb, an adjective, or another adverb.
- She drives **fast**.
- She is **very** pretty.
- She drives **very** fast.

Though many adverbs end in -*ly*, some do not. Therefore, use a dictionary when you are not sure of the form of an adverb.

If clauses to express future meaning

If you're hungry, I'**ll make** you a sandwich.

If it's sunny, we'**ll go** to the park.

If I have enough money, I'**m going to** buy that computer.

If Kim isn't well, she **won't** come to the party.

Remember: Use the present tense in the *if* clause. Use the future tense in the main clause. An *if* clause can come before or after a main clause.

If you're hungry, I'll make you a sandwich.

I'll make you a sandwich **if you're hungry**.

Practice

Adjectives and adverbs of manner

1 Answer the questions using an adverb.
Write complete sentences. Use the cues.

1. Why is Madonna popular?

   (*sing / good*) <u>She's popular because she</u>
   <u>sings well.</u>

2. Why do the children like the park?

   (*can play / happy*) _____ there.

3. Why is Ms. Burgess a good English teacher?

   (*speak / clear*) _____

4. Why isn't Monica a good driver?

   (*drive / dangerous*) _____

5. Why are they always tired?

   (*get up / early*) _____

6. Why is Tony a good student?

   (*study / hard*) _____

7. Why is Doreen a good assistant?

   (*type / fast*) _____

8. Why do you like her children?

   (*behave / polite*) _____

2 Rewrite the sentences. Change the adjectives to adverbs and the adverbs to adjectives.

1. Paul and Molly can run fast.

   Paul and Molly are fast runners.

2. She is an energetic tennis player.

   She plays tennis energetically.

3. Sally is a good guitar player.

   _____

4. My dad is a safe driver.

   _____

5. Some students learn quickly.

   _____

6. José speaks fluent English.

   _____

7. You write skillfully.

   _____

8. He is a patient listener.

   _____

9. Our president speaks effectively.

   _____

Practice

If clauses to express future meaning

3 Mr. Gomez is thinking about his summer vacation in Hawaii.
Match the two halves of each sentence. Write the letters.

___e___ 1. If the weather is sunny,   a. I'll find a better one.

_____ 2. If it rains,   b. I'll swim in the ocean.

_____ 3. If the hotel isn't good,   c. I'll call home often.

_____ 4. If renting a car is cheap,   d. I'll rent a big car.

_____ 5. If I need exercise,   e. I'll walk on the beach
                                                every day.
_____ 6. If international calls
         aren't expensive,   f. I'll stay in the hotel.

4 Complete each sentence. Circle the correct form of the verb.

1. I ((will make)/ make) you a sandwich if you're hungry.

2. If you (will be / are) late for school, you'll get into trouble.

3. If we (won't run / don't run), we'll miss the bus.

4. If it snows tomorrow, I ('m going to go / go) snowboarding.

5. I ('ll clean / clean) your windows if you give me five dollars.

6. My mom gets mad if I (won't get / don't get) good grades.

7. If it's too expensive, we (won't stay / don't stay) at The Ritz.

8. You'll lose your friends if you (won't be / aren't) honest with them.

9. If your friend drives carefully, I ('ll ride / ride) with him.

10. Don't worry. My dog won't bite you if he (will like / likes) you.

5 Complete the sentences using the verbs in parentheses. Use the simple present tense and the future tense. Use contractions when possible.

1. If I _____see_____ Sue, I _'ll give_____ her your message. (see / give)

2. Jim _____ annoyed if we _____ late again. (be / be)

3. You _____ hungry if you _____ any breakfast. (be / not, eat)

4. I _____ very surprised if you _____ the test. (be / not, pass)

5. If you _____ a party, I _____ you all my CDs. (have / lend)

6. If she _____ soon, I _____ without her. (not, arrive / go)

7. If he _____ well, I _____ the doctor. (not, feel / call)

8. I _____ if I _____ another cup of coffee. (not, sleep / drink)

Practice

6 Match a line in Column A with a line from Column B to write sentences with *if* clauses expressing a future condition.

A

1. it / stop snowing
2. you / wash the dishes
3. she / not like the food
4. the phone / ring
5. you / like scary movies
6. he / not study hard
7. I / get a raise at work
8. he / go to the gym more often

B

a. I / buy a new TV
b. we / go for a walk
c. you / love *Nightmare*
d. I / dry them
e. he / not pass his exams
f. he / lose a lot of weight
g. I / answer it
h. she / not finish the dinner

1. *If it stops snowing, we'll go for a walk.*
2. _____
3. _____
4. _____
5. _____
6. _____
7. _____
8. _____

7 Imagine that the situations listed in the chart are going to happen to you. In your notebook, write a sentence telling what will happen in each situation. Use *if* clauses.

What will happen if . . .
• your teacher doesn't give you any homework tonight?
• you break your leg?
• you don't get home before midnight tonight?
• you don't eat lunch?
• you get tickets to see your favorite band?
• there's a thunderstorm on your way home?

Example:
If my teacher doesn't give me any homework tonight, I'll go to the movies with my friends.

Unit 7

Grammar Highlights

The present perfect for the indefinite past

Affirmative statements

I **have** (I**'ve**) **seen** that movie twice.
He **has** (He**'s**) **eaten** there once or twice.

Yes/No questions

Have you **watched** this vido?
Has she **ever traveled** there?

Negative statements

I **have not** (**haven't**) **read** that book.
She **has never listened** to that CD.

Short answers

Yes, I **have**. / No, I **haven't**.
Yes, she **has**. / No, she **hasn't**.

Remember:
• Use *have* or *had* and the past participle to form the present perfect.
• Use the present perfect to talk about things that happened at some indefinite time in the past.
• You can use *ever* with the present perfect in questions.
• You can use *never* with the present perfect in negative answers.

The present perfect with *for* and *since*

For

They've been gone **for** three months.
I've had this dress **for** about three years.

Since

She has been our teacher **since** May.
I've played the piano **since** February 2003.

Information questions

How long have you lived there?

Short answers

For two years.
Since 2002.

Remember:
• Use *for* and a length of time to say how long a situation lasted.
• Use *since* and a point in time to say when something began.
• Use *how long* with the present perfect for questions.

Practice

The present perfect for the indefinite past

1 Read the postcard. Underline all the examples
of the present perfect tense.

Dear Carla,   July 10, ——

We are having a great vacation here in
Paris. We <u>'ve seen</u> lots of fantastic sights.
We've been to some great art galleries, and
we've met some really nice people. Mom and
Dad have left us on our own today, so we can
do whatever we want. I think I'll climb up the
Eiffel Tower — I haven't done that yet. Sara
says she wants to go to the Cathedral of Notre
Dame (she's seen the Disney movie about the
hunchback, and she's curious about it). I've
decided not to go with her, but I haven't told
her yet. I hope she won't be upset! Have you
heard about our grades yet? What about
Juan? Has he written to you? Why don't you
e-mail me with your news? There is a computer
at the hotel that guests can use, but I
haven't tried it yet.

Take care.

Milo

2 Complete the sentences. Write the present perfect of the verbs from the box.
Use contractions when possible.

| finish   read   go   eat   lose   see   ~~write~~   speak   take |

1. Why don't you answer her letters?
   She <u>'s written</u> to you three times!

2. He's a terrific actor. I _____ all his
   movies.

3. We _____ lunch at this restaurant
   many times.

4. He _____ to Jane on the phone a few
   times since she moved away.

5. Diego _____ to the beach. He should
   be back soon.

6. She has an excellent camera. She _____
   some beautiful photos over the years.

7. I _____ my keys. Can you open the
   door for me, please?

8. She _____ every book Hemingway
   ever wrote.

9. We _____ our work. Can we go out
   now?

Practice

3 Complete the second part of the sentences. Use the verbs from the first part. Write the negative form of the present perfect tense.

1. I made seven cups of coffee yesterday, but I <u>haven't made</u> any today.

2. Lucy took a lot of photos yesterday, but she _____ any today.

3. We saw a lot of movies last week, but we _____ any this week.

4. I wore these shoes last year, but I _____ them this year.

5. He exercised yesterday, but he _____ today.

6. They worked hard last year, but they _____ hard this year.

7. He lost a lot of money last week, but he _____ any this week.

8. We wrote a lot of postcards last summer, but we _____ any this summer.

9. She came here often last year, but this year she _____ here very often.

10. He played tennis every day last year, but this year he _____ it much.

11. There was a lot of sun last month, but there _____ any sun this month.

4 Complete the sentences. Write the present perfect tense of the verbs in parentheses. Use contractions when possible.

I am 84 years old, and I (*live*) <u>'ve lived</u>(1) a very interesting life. I (*have*) _____(2) lots of different jobs, and I (*travel*) _____(3) to many different countries. My older brother is 94 years old, but he (*not / be*) _____(4) to as many countries as I have. In fact, he (*not / leave*) _____(5) his hometown in more than 50 years! We're good friends, though. We (*not / fight*) _____(6) since the 1950s! Next year we're going on vacation together. I (*not / have*) _____(7) a real vacation because I (*work*) _____(8) all my life. We're going to Florida. I was there once, but I was working as a waiter then. This time I'm going to have fun!

Practice

5 Write *Yes/No* questions for the statements. Then write short answers, using the information.

1. Lauren has been a key pal before.

   Has Lauren ever been a key pal before?

   Yes, she has.

2. I've never seen that movie.

   _____

   _____

3. He's tried to fix that game twice.

   _____

   _____

4. We've never played on a basketball team before.

   _____

   _____

5. They've bought CDs at that music store before.

   _____

   _____

6. Daniel has gone to that beach many times.

   _____

   _____

7. Paula has never been to my house.

   _____

   _____

The present perfect with *for* and *since*

6 Complete the sentences with the present perfect tense of the verb in parentheses and *for* or *since*. Write the answers in the blanks.

1. We __*'ve lived*__ in this house
   ___(live)___

   __*for*__ ten years.
   ___(for / since)___

2. Wow! You _____ in the library
   ___(be)___

   _____ 1:00 P.M.
   ___(for / since)___

3. Marco _____ in that store
   ___(shop)___

   _____ last summer.
   ___(for / since)___

4. Odessa _____ _____ three
   ___(rollerskate)___   ___(for / since)___

   years.

5. I _____ dance lessons _____
   ___(take)___   ___(for / since)___

   last year.

6. She _____ him _____ the
   ___(like)___   ___(for / since)___

   last three months.

7. Leon _____ in my computer class
   ___(be)___

   _____ March.
   ___(for / since)___

8. Ashley and Tyler _____ the drums
   ___(play)___

   _____ last winter.
   ___(for / since)___

9. They _____ their dog _____
   ___(have)___   ___(for / since)___

   May.

10. Both Mr. and Mrs. Bryant _____
    ___(teach)___

    English _____ the last ten years.
    ___(for / since)___

Unit 8

Grammar Highlights

The present perfect with *yet* and *already*

Affirmative statements with *already*

We**'ve already seen** that movie.
I've **already listened** to that CD.

Negative statements with *yet*

We **haven't seen** that movie yet.
I **haven't listened** to that CD yet.

Yes/No questions with yet

Have you **asked** your teacher about your grade **yet**?
Has she **finished** her book report **yet**?

Short answers

Yes, I **have**. / No, I **haven't**.
Yes, she **has**. / No, she **hasn't**.

The present perfect contrasted with the simple past

The present perfect

I**'ve written** that report already.
We**'ve listened** to those CDs twice.
He **hasn't bought** that book yet.

The simple past

She **wrote** that report yesterday.
You **listened** to those CDs last night.
He **didn't buy** that book last week.

> **Remember:**
> • Use the present perfect for activities that happened at an indefinite time in the past.
> • Use the simple past for activities that were completed at a specific time in the past.

Adjective clauses with *who*, *that*, and *where*

Mrs. Brown is the woman **who shouted at my sister**.
The girl **that I told you about** is over there.
I didn't like the bike **that I bought**.
The office **where she works** is very close.

> **Remember:**
> • A clause has a subject and a verb. An adjective clause describes or gives more information about a noun. It comes after the noun it describes. An adjective clause is called a dependent clause because it cannot stand alone as a sentence.
> • *Who* refers to people; *where* refers to places; *that* can refer to people, places, or things.

Practice

The present perfect with *yet* and *already*

1 Look at the chart. Ask questions about what the people have done today. Then write short answers. Use *yet* and the cues.

	Watch the news	Eat breakfast	Read the newspaper	Do homework	Wash the dishes
Rita	✓	X	X	X	✓
Paulo and Sue	X	✓	X	✓	✓
You					

1. Rita / watch the news
   Has Rita watched the news yet?
   Yes, she has.

2. Paulo and Sue / watch the news
   Have Paulo and Sue watched the news yet?
   No, they haven't.

3. Rita / eat breakfast
   _____
   _____

4. Paulo and Sue / read newspaper
   _____
   _____

5. Rita / do homework
   _____
   _____

6. Paulo and Sue / wash dishes
   _____
   _____

7. Rita / read newspaper
   _____
   _____

8. Paulo and Sue / do homework
   _____
   _____

9. Rita / wash dishes
   _____
   _____

10. Paulo and Sue / eat breakfast
    _____
    _____

2 Complete the chart in Exercise 1 with information about what you have and haven't done today. Then write five true sentences. Use *already* and *yet*. Use contractions when possible.

Examples: *I've already watched the news.*

   I haven't watched the news yet.

1. _____
2. _____
3. _____
4. _____
5. _____

Practice

The present perfect vs. the simple past

3 Complete the sentences using the cues. Write the simple past or the present perfect tense of the verbs in parentheses.

Laura: (1. *you / see*) _Did you see_ *The Grove* last night?

Chloe: No, I didn't. I (2. *not / watch*) _____ TV for a long time! What (3. *happen*) _____ since Kate got married? (4. *she / have*) _____ a baby yet?

Laura: Yes. She (5. *have*) _____ a baby three weeks ago!

Chloe: What about Brett and Kylie? (6. *they / start*) _____ going out yet?

Laura: Brett and Kylie (7. *not / be*) _____ in *The Grove* recently.

Chloe: Why not?

Laura: They (8. *have*) _____ a terrible car accident on Kylie's birthday, and Brett (9. *die*) _____.

Chloe: That's awful. What (10. *Kylie / do*) _____ after the accident?

Laura: She (11. *go*) _____ back to Australia. She (12. *not / want*) _____ to stay in the United States.

Chloe: (13. *Chris / leave*) _____ his wife yet?

Laura: Yes. In fact, he (14. *already / find*) _____ another woman! They (15. *meet*) _____ on an airplane.

Chloe: (16. *old Mrs. Moreton / die*) _____ yet?

Laura: No. She's very happy right now because her son, Liam (17. *just / come*) _____ back from England. Why don't you come and watch it with me tonight?

Chloe: I don't have time. I'll call you tomorrow for the latest news!

Adjective clauses with *who*, *that*, and *where*

4 Complete the sentences with *who*, *that*, or *where*.

1. I have a cat _that_ likes eating vegetables.

2. The bedroom is a place _____ I relax and listen to music.

3. She goes to a school _____ has a lot of rules.

4. There's a boy in my class _____ plays the guitar in a band.

5. I don't like wearing clothes _____ are not fashionable.

6. The café _____ we usually meet is closed.

7. A soccer fan is a person _____ supports a soccer team.

8. Do you know anyone _____ wants to buy an old stereo?

9. Australia is a country _____ many unusual animals live.

10. Did you see the movie _____ won all those Oscars?

Practice

5 Match the main clauses with the adjective clauses. Write the letters.
Then write sentences on the lines below using *who*, *that*, or *where*.

_a_ 1. A stadium is a place	a. people play sports.
____ 2. A nurse is a person	b. fixes cars.
____ 3. A dishwasher is a machine	c. you wear on your feet.
____ 4. A dentist is a person	d. takes care of sick people.
____ 5. Socks are items of clothing	e. you can find many books.
____ 6. A library is a place	f. cleans dishes.
____ 7. A mechanic is a person	g. takes care of teeth.

1. _A stadium is a place where people play sports._
2. _____
3. _____
4. _____
5. _____
6. _____
7. _____

6 Combine the sentences using *who*, *that*, or *where*.
(You might need to delete words.)

1. Tom Cruise is an actor. He stars in many movies.
   Tom Cruise is an actor who stars in many
   movies.

2. Sprint is a new shop. It sells sports clothes for young people.
   _____

3. The Picasso is a café. Young people like to hang out there.
   _____

4. Chococrunch is a new chocolate bar. It contains nuts.
   _____

5. Passion is a new dance club. Teenagers go dancing there.
   _____

6. LemKool is a healthy drink. It gives you energy.
   _____

7. Power is a new health club. People go there to work out.
   _____

8. Jennifer Lopez is a famous singer. She acts in movies, too.
   _____

Unit 9

Grammar Highlights

Comparative and superlative forms of regular adjectives

Positive	Comparative	Superlative	Spelling rules
warm	warm**er than**	**the** warm**est**	For most one-syllable adjectives, add -*er* to form the comparative or -*est* to form the superlative.
big	big**ger than**	**the** big**gest**	For one-syllable adjectives that end in one vowel and one consonant, double the consonant and then add -*er* to form the comparative or -*est* to form the superlative.
happy	happ**ier than**	**the** happ**iest**	For two-syllable adjectives that end in -*y*, change the -*y* to an -*i* and add -*er* to form the comparative or -*est* to form the superlative.
famous	**more** famous **than**	**the most** famous	For other two-syllable adjectives, use *more* to form the comparative or *the most* to form the superlative.
serious	**more** serious than	**the most** serious	For adjectives with three or more syllables, use *more* to form the comparative and *the most* to form the superlative.

Comparative and superlative forms of irregular adjectives

Positive	Comparative	Superlative
good	**better than**	**the best**
bad	**worse than**	**the worst**
far	**farther than**	**the farthest**

Remember:
- Use the comparative to compare two people, places, and things.
- Use the superlative to compare one person, place, or thing to two or more other people, places, and things.
- You can also use *less than* or *the least* to compare things.
  Skiing is **less dangerous than** snowboarding.
  This novel is **the least interesting** book I've ever read.
- *Less* means the opposite of *more*. *Least* means the opposite of *most*.

Making comparisons with *as . . . as / not as . . . as*

The dessert was **as good as** the main course.
The soup was **not as good as** the salad.

Remember:
- Use *as* + adjective + *as* to say that there is no difference between two people or things.
- Use *not as* + adjective + *as* to say that there is a difference between two people or things.

Practice

Comparative and superlative forms of regular adjectives

1 Complete the sentences. Write the comparative and the superlative forms of the adjectives in parentheses.

1. (*big*) John's car is *bigger than* Mary's car, but Mark's car is *the biggest*.

2. (*warm*) The living room is _____ the kitchen, but the bedroom is _____.

3. (*funny*) Your joke was _____ mine, but his joke was _____.

4. (*interesting*) I think English is _____ geography, but biology is _____.

5. (*fat*) The black cat is _____ the white one, but the gray cat is _____.

6. (*young*) John is _____ Mario, but Stefan is _____.

7. (*comfortable*) This bed is _____ your bed, but that bed is _____.

8. (*heavy*) Your bag is _____ my bag, but Dad's bag is _____.

9. (*nice*) Tom's girlfriend is _____ your girlfriend, but my girlfriend is _____.

10. (*busy*) Yesterday was _____ today, but Friday was _____.

Comparative and superlative forms of irregular adjectives

2 Complete the sentences. Write the comparative or the superlative forms of the adjectives in the box.

good	bad	far

1. A: What a terrible movie! I think it was *the worst* movie I've ever seen.

   B: I disagree. I think *Lost in the Desert* was _____ that one.

2. A: Shakira is wonderful. She is _____ Britney Spears.

   B: No way! Britney Spears is _____ singer and dancer in the world!

3. Martin threw the javelin _____ Sean did. But Gregor won the gold medal because he threw the javelin _____.

3 Write sentences expressing your opinions. Use the cues and superlative forms of the adjectives *good* or *bad*.

1. actor / good
   Robert De Niro is the best actor in the world.

2. actor / bad
   _____

3. singer / good
   _____

4. singer / bad
   _____

5. movie / good
   _____

6. movie / bad
   _____

Practice

More . . . than, less . . . than, the most . . . , the least . . .

4 Look at the chart. Complete the comparative and superlative sentences for each adjective in the chart. Use *more . . . than, less . . . than, the most . . . ,* and *the least . . .* in the sentences. Use item 1 as a model.

YOUR GUIDE TO THE BEST DANCE CLUBS	Dr. Frank's	The Garage	Secrets
1. crowded	* * *	* *	*
2. expensive	*	* *	* * *
3. exciting	* * *	* *	*
4. popular	* * *	* *	*
5. interesting music	* * *	* *	*

1. The Garage <u>is more crowded than Secrets</u>
<u>but less crowded than Dr. Frank's</u>.

   Dr. Frank's is <u>the most crowded</u> of the clubs.

   Secrets is <u>the least crowded</u> of the clubs.

2. The Garage is _____
   _____.

   Dr. Frank's is _____ of the clubs.

   Secrets is _____ of the clubs.

3. The Garage is _____
   _____.

   Secrets is _____ of the clubs.

   Dr. Frank's is _____ of the clubs.

4. The Garage is _____
   _____.

   Dr. Frank's is _____ of the clubs.

   Secrets is _____ of the clubs.

5. The Garage has _____
   _____.

   Dr. Frank's has _____ of the clubs.

   Secrets has _____ of the clubs.

Not as . . . as

5 Read the sentences in Column A. Then write new sentences using the adjectives in Column B and *not as . . . as*.

A

1. Turtles are slower than rabbits.
2. This book is worse than that book.
3. Science is more boring than geography.
4. Julio's house is smaller than Marco's.
5. This restaurant is less crowded than that restaurant.
6. Regular wrestlers are weaker than Sumo wrestlers.
7. Ahmed is funnier than Hamid.
8. Jill's children are younger than Rita's.
9. Marisa Tomei is less well known than Julia Roberts.

B

1. *(fast)*
2. *(good)*
3. *(interesting)*
4. *(big)*
5. *(busy)*
6. *(strong)*
7. *(serious)*
8. *(old)*
9. *(famous)*

1. <u>Turtles are not as fast as rabbits.</u>
2. _____
3. _____
4. _____
5. _____
6. _____
7. _____
8. _____
9. _____

Practice

The comparative form of adjectives; *as . . . as*; *not as . . . as*

6 Read the information under each set of pictures. Then write comparative sentences using the cues and a comparative adjective, *as . . . as*, or *not as . . . as*.

1.

   today (98°F)   **yesterday (93°F)**

   (*hot*) Today ___is hotter than yesterday___.

2.

   giant pandas   **Sumatran rhinos**
   (about 1,100 left)   **(about 300 left)**

   (*endangered*) Giant pandas ___are not as___
   ___endangered as Sumatran rhinos___.

3.

   gymnast   **basketball player**
   (4'10")   **(6'8")**

   (*tall*) The gymnast _____
   _____.

4.

   Ferrari ($150,000)   **Porsche ($80,000)**

   (*expensive*) A Ferrari _____
   _____.

5.

   blue whales   **elephants**
   (150 tons)   **(5 tons)**

   (*heavy*) Blue whales _____
   _____.

6.

   cheetahs   **racehorses**
   (70 miles per hour)   **(45 miles per hour)**

   (*fast*) Cheetahs _____
   _____.

7.

   turkey sandwiches   **ham sandwiches**
   ($4 each)   **($4 each)**

   (*expensive*) The turkey sandwiches _____
   _____.

Grammar Highlights

The past continuous: statements

I **was working** at four o'clock yesterday afternoon.
They **were making dinner** *when* the police knocked on the door.
While Tina **was sunbathing**, someone stole her purse.
While Tina **was sunbathing**, we **were sitting** in the cafe.

Remember:
- Use the past continuous to describe an action in progress at a specific time in the past.
- Use the *when* clause to describe something that happened at a specific time in the past. Use the simple past in the *when* clause.
- Use the *while* clause to describe something that was happening at the same time something else happened. Use the past continuous in the *while* clause.
- When two actions are in progress at the same time, use the past continuous in both clauses.

The past continuous: information questions

Wh- word	*was/were*	subject	verb + *-ing*	*when* or *while* clause
What	**were**	they	**making**	**when** the police came?
Where	**was**	Tina	**sunbathing**?	
What	**were**	you	**doing**	**while** Tina was sunbathing?

Who	*was*	verb + *-ing*		
Who	**was**	**sleeping**	at 5 P.M.?	

Practice

The past continuous: statements

1 Read the sentences. Then decide which action started first, a or b. Circle the letter.

1. It was raining when I started the car.

   (a.) It started to rain.
   b. I started the car.

2. When we arrived at the stadium, the players were running onto the field.

   a. We arrived at the stadium.
   b. The players started to run onto the field.

3. David saw a lion while he was traveling in Africa.

   a. David saw the lion.
   b. David went to Africa.

4. While we were watching TV, a bird flew in through the window.

   a. We started watching TV.
   b. A bird flew in through the window.

5. Alan was skateboarding when he sprained his ankle.

   a. He got on his skateboard.
   b. He sprained his ankle.

6. The burglar escaped through the window while the police were trying to open the door.

   a. The burglar escaped through the window.
   b. The police tried to open the door.

7. When the ambulance arrived, the injured man was feeling better.

   a. The ambulance arrived.
   b. The injured man began to feel better.

8. I opened a can of soda while my parents were sunbathing by the pool.

   a. I opened a can of soda.
   b. My parents lay down by the pool.

9. When Sandra arrived, I was cooking dinner.

   a. I started cooking dinner.
   b. Sandra arrived.

2 Combine the two sentences in different ways. Use *when* and *while*. Write your sentences in your notebook.

1. I was working on my computer. The fire alarm sounded.

   a. When *the fire alarm sounded, I was working on my computer* .

   b. _____ while _____ .

   c. _____ when _____ .

2. Simon was driving home. He ran out of gas.

   a. While _____ .

   b. _____ when _____ .

3. I walked into the restaurant. Everybody stopped talking.

   a. When _____ .

   b. _____ when _____ .

4. Nina was studying. Her boyfriend called.

   a. While _____ .

   b. _____ while _____ .

   c. When _____ .

   d. _____ when _____ .

5. Greg was flying to Brazil. He heard the good news on the radio.

   a. While _____ .

   b. _____ while _____ .

   c. When _____ .

   d. _____ when _____ .

Practice

3 Write the sentences correctly. Put each verb in parentheses in the past continuous or simple perfect.

1. While she (*get*) ready to dive, a little boy (*push*) her into the water.

   While she was getting ready to dive, a little

   boy pushed her into the water.

2. He (*drive*) very fast when he (*hit*) the other car.

   _____

3. The phone (*ring*) while we (*watch*) a show about surfing.

   _____

4. She (*wait*) to pay for her groceries when somebody (*steal*) her car.

   _____

5. I (*not / go*) very fast when I (*fall*) off my bicycle.

   _____

6. Our CD player (*break*) while we (*listen*) to the music.

   _____

7. I (*live*) in Spain when I (*meet*) my girlfriend.

   _____

8. She (*dance*) when she (*slip*) and (*hurt*) her wrist.

   _____

9. The dog (*take*) my hamburger while I (*not / look*).

   _____

10. I (*open*) the curtains when I (*see*) my neighbor standing in the yard.

    _____

11. Sabrina (*eat*) her sandwich when she (*bite*) into something very hard.

    _____

12. Stuart (*see*) his teacher while he (*shop*) at the mall.

    _____

13. I (*feel*) the house shake as I (*take*) a shower.

    _____

14. The birds (*sing*), the sun (*shine*), and I (*relax*) on the grass. Suddenly I (*hear*) people yelling loudly. I (*jump*) up to see what (*happen*).

    _____

    _____

    _____

Practice

4 Complete the story below. Write the simple past or the past continuous tense of each verb in parentheses.

Last weekend, my brother (*invite*)

_____*invited*_____ three friends to our house. They
     (1)

(*play*) _____ a very noisy game, so I
          (2)

(*decide*) _____ to do my homework in the
           (3)

park. I (*find*) _____ a bench in a quiet
              (4)

place and (*sit*) _____ down.
                 (5)

I (*write*) _____ the first sentence of my
           (6)

English essay when a woman (*sit down*)

_____ next to me. She (*open*) _____
   (7)   **(8)**

a bag and (*start*) _____ to throw pieces of
                   (9)

bread on the ground. Suddenly, there were

about 30 birds around us. They (*make*)

_____ a terrible noise, so I (*stop*)
   (10)

_____ writing and (*put*) _____ my
   (11)   **(12)**

notebook and pen down on the ground.

I (*watch*) _____ the birds and (*think*)
            (13)

_____ about my essay when a boy (*skate*
   (14)

by) _____ very fast. He (*skate*) _____
      (15)   **(16)**

over my pen and (*break*) _____ it. I (*not /*
                          (17)

have) _____ another pen so I (*have*)
        (18)

_____ to go home to finish my
   (19)

homework.

The past continuous: information questions

5 Write questions about the story in Exercise 4. Use the cues.

1. What / her brother's friends / do / when / she / decide / to work in the park
   What were her brother's friends doing when
   she decided to work in the park?

2. Where / she / sit / when / she / start / to write her essay
   _____

3. Why / the birds / make a lot of noise
   _____

4. Who / feed / the birds
   _____

5. Who / skate by / while / she / think / about her essay
   _____

6 Write answers to the questions in Exercise 5.

1. *They were playing a noisy game.*
2. _____
3. _____
4. _____
5. _____

Unit 11

Grammar Highlights

The passive voice: present tense

Affirmative statements

The ice cream **is made** here.
The plates **are kept** in the cabinet.

Negative statements

The ice cream **is not made** here.
The plates **are not kept** in the cabinet.

Remember:
- Use the active voice to emphasize the subject of the sentence as the performer of the action.
- Use the passive voice to emphasize the subject of the sentence as the receiver of the action.
- Form the passive voice by using a form of the verb *be* and a past participle.
  My mother drives my brother to school every day.
  My brother **is driven** to school by my mother every day.
- Omit the *by* phrase in a passive sentence when the listener or speaker does not need to know the performer of the action.
  My brother **is driven** to school every day.

Practice

The passive voice: present tense

1 Read the sentences. Write *A* if the sentence is active; write *P* if it is passive. Underline the verbs that are in the passive voice.

_P_ 1. Garbage <u>is collected</u> once a week.

___ 2. The tickets for tonight's concert are sold out.

___ 3. We arrived on time.

___ 4. These shoes are imported from Brazil.

___ 5. She isn't sad.

___ 6. My grandfather built this house by himself.

___ 7. These houses are built from brick.

___ 8. Mail isn't delivered on Sunday.

___ 9. They get to work by car.

___10. Polar bears aren't found in Africa.

___11. The kids broke the window in the kitchen.

2 Complete each sentence below. Choose the correct verb from the box. Then write it using the passive voice in the simple present tense.

grow	leave	keep	make	show
~~eat~~	display	teach	sell	use

1. Usually, hot dogs ___*are eaten*___ with mustard in the United States.

2. A drive-in is an open-air theater where movies _____.

3. In most zoos, the animals _____ in cages.

4. Oranges _____ in California.

5. Books _____ in bookstores.

6. In some parts of Australia, there are no schools, and children _____ by radio.

7. Sometimes, dogs _____ by the police to catch criminals.

8. An art gallery is a place where pictures _____.

9. Cheese _____ from milk.

10. Every year, thousands of umbrellas _____ on trains.

3 Write sentences using the passive voice. Use the cues.

1. the windows / not clean / very often
   The windows aren't cleaned very often.

2. this shampoo / not test / on animals
   _____

3. this newspaper / read / by two million people every day
   _____

4. paper / make / from trees
   _____

5. a lot of electronics goods / produce / in Japan
   _____

6. the world's finest chocolate / make / in Belgium
   _____

7. the same stories / tell / all over the world
   _____

8. Spanish / speak / in many countries
   _____

Practice

4 Rewrite the sentences using the passive voice in the present tense.
Leave out the words in parentheses.

ALL ABOUT RICE

Did you know that half the people in the world eat rice every day?

Here are more facts about rice.

1. (The world) produces about three hundred and eighty million tons of rice a year.
   Three hundred and eighty million tons of rice are produced a year.

2. (You) need warm, wet weather to grow rice.
   _____

3. (They) grow and eat seventy percent of the world's rice in Asia.
   _____

4. (People) plant most of the world's rice by hand.
   _____

5. In Japan and in the United States, (they) use machines to harvest the rice.
   _____

6. At weddings, (people) throw rice at the newly married couple.
   _____

Practice

5 Look at the pictures. Then number the sentences below to show the correct sequence for performing the trick. Last, rewrite the sentences with the passive voice in the present tense.

HOW IS IT DONE?

___ He cuts the box into two pieces.

___ The magician takes the closed box onto the stage.

___ He opens the box to show the unhurt assistant.

_1_ Before the show, the magician asks an assistant to lie inside the box.

___ He amazes the audience.

___ He asks another assistant to lie inside the box.

1. *Before the show, an assistant is asked to lie*
   inside the box.

2. _____
   _____

3. _____
   _____

4. _____
   _____

5. _____
   _____

6. _____
   _____

Unit 12

Reflexive pronouns

Subject		Reflexive pronoun	Example
I	→	myself	I hurt **myself**.
he	→	himself	**He** hurt **himself**.
she	→	herself	**She** hurt **herself**.
it	→	itself	**The cat** washed **itself**.
you	→	yourself/yourselves	Be careful or **you**'ll hurt **yourself/yourselves**.
we	→	ourselves	**We** hurt **ourselves**.
they	→	themselves	**They** hurt **themselves**.

Remember: A reflexive pronoun is a pronoun that ends in -*self* (or -*selves*). It refers back to the subject of the sentence.

Gerund as subject / Gerund as object of a verb

Subject (gerund)	verb		Subject	verb	object (gerund)
Reading	is	fun.	I	enjoy	**reading**.

Gerund as object of a preposition

Subject	verb	preposition	object (gerund)
She	is thinking	of	**traveling**.

These verbs can be followed by gerunds:

admit	consider	feel like	keep on (continue)	mind	prefer
avoid	discuss	finish	like	miss	stop
begin	enjoy	hate	love	practice	suggest
can't help	explain	imagine			

Remember: A gerund (the base form of the verb + -*ing*) is a verb that functions as a noun. A gerund can be used as the subject of a sentence, as the object of a verb, or as the object of a preposition.

Practice

Reflexive pronouns

1 Match each question or statement with its reply. Write the letter.

_c_ 1. May I borrow your pen?

___ 2. We're going to Disneyland!

___ 3. Who painted their room?

___ 4. Who taught you how to draw?

___ 5. Who are you talking to?

___ 6. Are you going to turn the computer off?

___ 7. Why is she crying?

___ 8. Who let you in?

a. I'm talking to myself.

b. Nobody. We let ourselves in.

c. Sure. Help yourself.

d. I think she hurt herself.

e. I taught myself.

f. They did it themselves.

g. Enjoy yourselves!

h. No, it'll turn itself off.

2 Complete each sentence. Circle the correct word in parentheses.

1. I really hurt (*me* / (*myself*)) when I fell off my bike. Luckily, an old man stopped to help (*me* / *myself*).

2. Why don't you ask (*her* / *herself*) why she looks at (*her* / *herself*) in the mirror all the time.

3. We had to introduce (*us* / *ourselves*) at the meeting because nobody knew (*us* / *ourselves*).

4. You don't have to ask if you want something to eat. I told (*you* / *yourself*) to help (*you* / *yourself*).

5. House plants are nice, but you have to take care of (*them* / *themselves*) because they can't take care of (*them* / *themselves*).

6. Don't do his homework for (*him* / *himself*)! He can do it (*him* / *himself*).

7. The car alarm will turn (*it* / *itself*) off if you leave (*it* / *itself*) alone.

8. When I saw (*me* / *myself*) in the mirror, I realized why people were looking at (*me* / *myself*) strangely.

Practice

Gerund as subject / Gerund as object

3 Complete the sentences. Write the gerund form of the verbs in parentheses.

1. (*learn*) ____Learning____ a foreign language often takes years of study.

2. (*watch*) _____ TV all day is not a good way to spend a vacation.

3. (*run*) _____ is good exercise.

4. (*listen*) _____ to music is my favorite free-time activity.

5. (*skateboard*) _____ is a very popular sport among teenagers.

6. (*earn*) _____ money from an after-school job is a great idea!

7. (*answer*) _____ the phone and (*write*) _____ letters is my assistant's job.

4 Rewrite the sentences. Use a gerund as the subject of each new sentence.

1. It is exciting to watch a good game of soccer.
   Watching a good game of soccer is exciting.

2. It is silly to worry about unimportant things.
   _____

3. It is fun to play games with my little brother.
   _____

4. It is easy to learn how to drive a car.
   _____

5. It is important to stay calm in an emergency.
   _____

6. It is uncomfortable to sit on the floor for too long.
   _____

7. It is expensive to fly to Paris on the Concorde.
   _____

5 Complete the sentences. Write the gerund form of the verbs from the box.

| dry | fail | ~~dance~~ | cook |
| move | give | leave | get |

1. Do you enjoy *dancing* in clubs?

2. Have you finished _____ dinner yet?

3. If you don't study, you'll keep on _____ your exams.

4. Do you mind _____ over a little?

5. It's hard to avoid _____ wet when you are in a canoe.

6. He's thinking about _____ his job to travel around Europe for a year.

7. Sam doesn't enjoy _____ the dishes.

8. I don't mind _____ Teresa a ride home after school.

8. It is easy to find an after-school job in my town.
   _____

9. It is exciting to play in a band.
   _____

10. It is difficult to learn some foreign languages.
    _____

Practice

6 Write sentences with true information about yourself. Use the cues and *dislike*, *enjoy*, or *not mind*.

1. My friends and I / play / video games
   My friends and I dislike playing video games.

2. I / get up / early in the morning
   _____

3. My dad / cook / dinner for our family
   _____

4. My friends / wait / in line
   _____

5. My mom / play / tennis
   _____

6. Our teacher / tell / stories in class
   _____

7 Rewrite the sentences using the words in bold type and gerunds.

1. Don't get sunburned when you are at the beach today.

   avoid

   Avoid getting sunburned when you are at
   the beach today.

2. My friends and I love to hang out at the mall.

   enjoy

   My friends and I enjoy hanging out at
   the mall.

3. Does it bother you when people talk during the movie?

   mind

   _____

   _____

4. The doctor told me to exercise three times a week.

   suggested

   _____

   _____

5. I find it impossible not to laugh at your jokes.

   can't help

   _____

   _____

6. Jerry broke Anita's bicycle.

   admitted

   _____

   _____

7. Molly wanted to go to the park, but she decided to go to the library instead.

   consider

   _____

   _____

8. All through dinner, they just argued about how to decorate their new house.

   keep on

   _____

   _____